The Best Four Year Vacation EVER!

By "Slicktor" Victor Robinson

"God, please forgive me for my four years of sinful pleasure." - Sir Cronin ZBT

Slicktor Victor Entertainment, LLC

Pennsylvania

Copyright © 2014 Victor Slicktor Robinson

All rights reserved. No part of this book may be reproduced or transmitted in any form or by any means, electronic or mechanical, including photocopying, recording, or by any information storage and retrieval system, without permission in writing from the publisher.

Published by Slicktor Victor Entertainment, LLC
4219 South Othello St.
Seattle, WA 98118

Victorslicktor@gmail.com
First Edition.

ISBN: 978-0-692-21648-4

Printed in the United States of America.

Disclaimer

This book is presented as a true story based on the personal experiences of the author, however, the reader is advised that the material in this book has been modified to protect the identities of all the people mentioned within.

This book is presented solely for entertainment and educational purposes and is not intended to represent or be used as an exhaustive resource on the hazards of college life, nor the hazards of being young and free. The information contained in this book is made available for illustrative purposes, explaining only one person's perspective on the experience of Life.

The author emphasizes this material is not offered as advice. It is highly recommended you seek the services of a competent professional before making any decisions regarding your business or personal affairs.

Best efforts have underscored the writing of this book, but the author makes no representations or warranties of any kind and assumes no liabilities of any kind with respect to the accuracy or completeness of the contents, and specifically disclaim any implied warranties of use for any particular purpose.

The author shall not be held liable or responsible to any person or entity with respect to any loss or incidental or consequential damages caused, or alleged to have been caused, directly or indirectly, by the information contained in this book, or disruption caused by errors or omissions, whether such errors or omissions result from negligence, accident, or any other cause.

Meet the Author

My name is "Slicktor" Victor Robinson. I'm a "Class of 2013" graduate from Johnson & Wales University in Providence, Rhode Island who studied Sports/Entertainment and Event Management. Originally from Newark, NJ and raised in the Poconos, PA, I currently reside in Seattle, WA where I landed my first career job right after college as a Director of Sales and Marketing.

After graduating in May 2013, I started my own business, Slicktor Victor Entertainment, LLC. My business opened with offering just clothing, but quickly developed and now targets all facets of the entertainment industry. Today, SVE has two musical artists, a scholarship/financial literacy program, a cheese cake service and now, an exciting new piece of literature. In addition to SVE, I enjoy partying with friends, working out, playing basketball and getting tattoos and piercings.

After writing this book, I'm already working on some spinoffs to go along with this project as well as putting together a show or movie so you can enjoy seeing each character on stage or screen. If you want to contact me and ask personal questions, feel free to reach out through my webpage, **Slicktorvictor.com**, or on any of my social media sites (@SlicktorVictor); I will gladly respond.

I hope you enjoy this book, and can take something of value from it.

Thank you,

"Slicktor" Victor Robinson

Acknowledgements

Many people have been influential throughout the last three months of creating this book.

First, I would like to thank my parents. Many people always start by thanking the Man above, but He brought you in this world and you brought me here, so thank you from the bottom of my heart for leading me with the knowledge and funding to be able to enjoy such a short but GREAT college experience. I know things got rocky at some points, but we pulled through and I want to say I love you both, Mom and Dad, and that your son made it; I've made history.

Next, I want to give a huge thanks to my boys, brothers, partners in crime, etc.: Muggs, P Money, Cheese, Turbs, Trups, and Milla for putting up with my crazy ass during our four years at JWU. We've had the greatest of times, from going out, selling/doing drugs, banging the same women, to fighting and making up later. College wouldn't have been the same at all if I didn't meet you crazy fucks. I love you all and let's "Fuck Up This World" boys.

Steph, Katina and Cassie, my road dogs, my "Bishes" and my sisters. I love you all and I'm happy I had the opportunity to spend four years of my life with you guys. You girls made college a wild experience and I will never forget it. Thanks for sticking with me while writing this book. I know my mass text and facetime calls get annoying sometimes, but you guys always fit me in your schedule. So I love you all and we will have a successful future together. P.S., my next book is on you guys!

ZBT, thanks for all the memories, boys. College was a fun ride knowing that I pledged the craziest fraternity. From rushing, the basement, bid night, cross night, to raving every weekend now. I love you all, you sick bastards, and no one can take any of your places in my heart. ZBT for life!

A shout out to my editor, Dr. Daniel Levine. Your expertise, enthusiasm, and dedication were invaluable to the success of this book.

Last, I want to thank everyone who I've had the pleasure of meeting while at JWU. My orientation buddies, you know who you all are, I love you all. It was like yesterday we were all talking about how we thought the four years would've been, and I can tell you NONE of us were right, because shit got REAL, real fast. But, through all the bullshit we stayed close. This goes for everyone I met in Prov whether you're a "Prov Local", which we all became (lol), or not. If we crossed paths, I want to thank you, because you guys all made this book possible. For anyone and everyone who attends/attended JWU from 09'-13' , thanks a lot, guys, and let's show America we're not the degenerates we were in college, as we are now all successful men and women.

New Books COMING SOON!

- Classy or Un-classy: Steph andCassie

- Behind the Scenes of "The Best Four Year Vacation EVER!"

- Sassy

- The Real Life of Slicktor Victor! #EXPOSED

Forewords

When college is over, what are you left with? Invigorating memories and a degree proving your accomplishments. Victor takes it a step further with "The Best Four Year Vacation Ever". When I initially heard of the book I thought, "His experiences at our university on paper for the world to see? How could all the partying, sex and drugs over a four-year period be accurately portrayed? Is that even legal?"

To say the least, it caught my attention. Well, Victor manages to do it in a captivating, refreshing approach. Everything is covered from the first day jitters to the last hoorah. I had the divine experience of being a part of the shenanigans that took place in the outlandish city of Providence. Let me tell you, from what I can remember, it was unequivocal to anything else I have or will ever experience. Staying up all night, getting in fights just because we could, insane amounts of drugs, constant partying... Victor and I would keep partying until our bodies wouldn't allow us to go any further. Even when we had nothing to do we found a way to push the limit. "The Best Four Year Vacation Ever" is truly a unique, well-delivered, documentation of one hell of a fucking ride! — **Muggs**

College to me was all about choices; some choose to eat PB&J's every day, while we were eating steak and lobster. Some choose to find friends by having the same shirt on with letters, while we became friends because of the mighty dollar. Because, regardless where you're from there's always a Version of you in some other town or state. And that was Slicktor; we connected off the jump from living across the hall in the dorms to today being best friends. Love you Kid and Keep doing your thing.

— **Turbs**

The best phrase I have to describe Victor is "one of a kind." He definitely is not like anyone I've ever met. We became friends (maybe a little more than that, ha) our freshman year of college when we lived in the same dorm building. Victor was always barging into me and my roommate's room like it was his own, and whether it was just for a second to say hi, or for a few hours to hang out, he ALWAYS made sure to stop by and "check in". He never failed to make me laugh either, always telling funny stories, cracking jokes, or making fun of someone.

Throughout our four years of college I was able to get to know Victor on a more personal level, and although we may have casually "hooked up" a few times, we still managed to keep our friendship separate. We grew apart a little bit when he pledged his fraternity and then transferred to the JWU Miami campus, but every time he came back to visit, it was like he never left. There was a time when I thought he was going down a dark path and started worrying about him, (which you will read about in the book, but in normal "Victor" fashion, he bounced right back to the funny, driven, outgoing friend I always knew and loved. We shared so many memories during our "four year vacation", most of which we both probably don't remember, and I'm so glad that even after graduation we still keep in touch. The fact that he wrote this book on his college experience doesn't surprise me at all. He is without a doubt one of the most interesting people I know, and hopefully you will agree with me after you finish this book. I'm so proud of you, Vic! Keep doing big things! **Love always, J<3**

Vic has always been an ultimate partier. You know when he went hard when he had no voice or he's passed out on someone's couch. I used to call him Mr. Wobbles when he's wasted because he's wobbling all over the place, from stumbling, to passing out in someone's girl's titties. I had a great time in college. Especially with my whole team, and if I could do this whole thing over, I would only change one thing, which would be to go even harder! – **Milla**

Slicktor Victor is that friend your parents warned you about. The kid turned out to be one of the craziest motherfucking wingmen I've come across in my college career. The kid is too real!
- **Cheese**

"One Love" Buddha, Vic and Carol...looking back over time, the day was here when we had to face that Victor was embarking on yet another new chapter in his life...

Suddenly, the things that we worked so hard to prepare him for became one of the most challenging times in our lives. The shopping, packing, lectures and the WHAT!!!! limo ride was short...Here we sit downtown Providence, RI, staring at a beautiful brick building , Johnson & Wales University, with a bunch of rambunctious young men and women moving in, around and about.

Then the do's and dont's lecture ~ the one thing that stuck out was "Don't call your child everyday" and my mouth opened with a WHAT!!! Then a tap on the shoulder with a masculine voice saying. "Okay, see you later!" Time to go...trying desperately to hold back the tears...separation. The ride home was long.

Thoughts of what do we do now? Seconds, minutes, hours, days seemed like forever. The 2:00 a.m. phone calls, spring breaks, pledging, fun times, good decisions and bad decisions ... time sits still for no one. Here we are...Graduation Day...May 2013 is here! WOW! A crowning moment and we were the proudest two people in the world. Victor lived, laughed and loved, crossed streams, oceans and shores. Now he is a young man whom we are extremely proud of, for his many accomplishments and paths chosen... and to be chosen. The sky is the limit and he's grabbing every star on the way up. Congratulations, Victor Darnell "Slicktor" Robinson. — **Love, Mom and Dad**

Table of Contents

Freshman Year:

- My First Day of Freedom — 14
- Party Time! — 19
- Setting the Pace — 26
- The Bitch Ass Pussies of Delta Upsilon — 38
- Pledging with the ZBT Maniacs — 47
- Spring Break in Miami — 58
- Back in Provi — 62
- Summertime, and the Living is Sleazy — 69

Sophomore Year:

- My Favorite Year of College! — 76
- Heading Downhill Fast — 85
- The Trip from Hell — 94
- Roofied on St. Patty's Day — 112
- Money Mike's Turn — 119
- The Summer Before Miami — 126

Junior Year:

- A Piece of Me   130
- Living in Magic City   134
- Making Magic   143
- Providence   151
- I Get Robbed ... and Lose My Girl   155
- Back in Prov   163

Senior Year:

- Stroking It   168
- Xanax Rules   174
- Crash!   180
- Little Miss Ugly   185
- The Emerald City   189
- The Boston Marathon Bombings   198
- The Vacation's About Over   200
- Shout Out   207
- The Meaning of Life   211
- Where We Are Today   213

Freshman Year

Chapter 1

My First Day of Freedom

The day was finally here. Freedom was so close! The long summer of waiting was over and I was about to drift into my new life.

Not that summer had been bad or anything; it was actually sick, with lots of parties, my crew and I raising hell, getting into some shady moments, sliding through the wet hot days of a Pennsylvania summer and chilling in the long cool evenings with the maple trees full of broad leaves, the blinking fireflies tripping me out with memories of when I was a kid and the summer stretched forever. And there had been Keisha, warm, soft, gentle Keisha to heat up the cool nights in my first summer after high school. Man, oh man, she had a body that gave and gave and gave...and I took.

That was before, and this was now. A whole new life was opening up for me and I was eager to see where and how far it was going to take me. I was excited! This was me, Victor Slicktor, living my life the way I wanted, and the only rules I worried about were the ones that could run faster than me.

I had met a bunch of cool bros and nice-looking ladies during the summer orientation at Johnson & Wales University, and we were all dialed in. I don't know how much you know about Johnson & Wales University, but it's the best party school on the East Coast. Most of the population at JW is rich kids mostly from the New England area or Long Island. JW has some of the hottest girls you'll see in the Northeast! Most kids go there only for the parties so they can get trashed and laid, out of range from their parents' eyes.

That's why I was going. I didn't give a fuck about the classes, because all I wanted to do was get away from my parents and have a good time. Oh sure, I registered for classes and had my first trimester worked out, but I had other things in mind.

The last week or 10 days before classes were starting there was a lot of buzz with me and my new friends texting each other. Everyone was talking online, saying they were bringing this down and that down, and I could feel the party mode slowly kick in and then turn into a torrent as each day brought us closer to the freedom we craved.

So it was almost time, and I've got my bags packed and the whole vision is in my head, me with new friends, unbelievably hot chicks, nonstop party time, living free and easy. And to make things flow until I can get hooked up, the night before I happened to pick up a massive amount of marijuana from one of my cousins, nearly a half kilo of some of the finest Pennsylvania bud anywhere. This shit smelled sweet! When I put my nose in the bag and took a deep breath, I got high from the fragrance! So I stashed this treasure in my bags. My mom and dad had ordered a limo to take the three of us to JW, and we were going to be leaving at 6:00 a.m. the next morning for the drive to Providence.

Holy shit! While I'm sleeping, my mom finds the stash in my bags... I wake up and soon we're leaving the house. I decide to stuff another shirt into my bag and it doesn't feel right. I quickly look for the stash, and it's not there! My mom was keeping an eye out and saw me looking through my bags, and she told me she had gone through my stuff, found it, took it, and flushed it all down the toilet!

Fucking Hell! All my royal smoke was gone and now I was heading off to college empty-handed. We get into the black limo and I was pissed, and I was pissed the entire six hour limo ride to Providence.

Even though the trip started with a black cloud, after a while I was diggin' it! I would soon be 300 miles from home. With every mile that limo rolled, my new horizon was coming up. I'd done the paperwork, paid the fees, made the visits, and now I was sailing into Johnson & Wales University in Providence, Rhode Island, for my first college trimester. My heart was bursting with excitement, and my mind was racing! I was almost free! Free from all the rules in my mom and dad's house, free to change my labels, drop the patterns, break the mold and become who I really was! I could do anything, and I was ready to do everything!

The limo pulled up in front of McNulty Hall, a big red-brick seven story dormitory. I'd been here before and I knew what to expect. It was a beautiful sunny New England day, with a few giant white clouds pinned in the big blue sky. There was just the edge of a soft breeze coming in from the bay and I knew I had come home.

And the women! Beautiful long legged college ladies in shorts or tight jeans and sandals were walking by, some with long straight hair, some with bushy brown hair, and bodies full of promise. I found myself falling in love with all of them!

So we're here, we're finally here. I'd been asleep the last hour and when I woke up I was feeling antsy, really edgy and antsy, and I remember feeling angry inside, too. I was just so ready to get out and get started, living on my own, you know? After years of rules and all the crap of high school, I'd had enough and I was totally ready to live on my own, getting out from underneath my parents. And then we pull up in front of the dorm and it was just like heaven.

It was way cool driving up in front of the dorm in this shiny black limousine. A couple of people were watching our limo arrive and they saw me getting out. I could see in their faces that they were asking, "Oh, man, who's this guy?", you know? It was a fun moment, pulling up to JW like a celebrity. Little did they know that I would be one.

Okay, so now we had to get all my shit into the dormitory and into my room. I didn't have a lot, but enough so that it took me, the limo driver, and Doudjy, my new roommate, two trips to get it all upstairs. My room was on the fourth floor, and as we're moving my stuff through the lobby and into the elevator, there is this amazing energy all around me... College kids everywhere, dudes of every kind; some were tall and buff, others were short, sloppy and fat; sandals, sneakers, shorts, slacks...

And the college girls were also swarming all around me, and every single one of them looked delicious and available. Some were athletic and had nice tight butts, some had little breasts lightly poking at their T-shirts, and other women had these big round breasts that were barely sheltered by their dipping blouses. I could almost feel that soft smooth sexy flesh in my hands. I was as hard as a rock thinking about all that luscious real estate, and I had to carry my stuff low so I wouldn't show while my mom and dad were around.

So we got all my shit into the room and now it's time to say goodbye to my parents, you know? It was a little sad as I watched my mom and dad walk down the pathway at Gaebe Commons where my dorm was, back to the waiting limo...and I could see my mom had started crying, so I felt this pain in my heart and I ran back down to give her a hug, and she was slobbering and I felt my throat swell up and I got teary, too, and so we hugged and I promised to call and Dad was looking strong but I could see he was unhappy, and we took pictures, and then they finally left.

I had arrived, and now was the beginning of my new life.

Chapter 2

Party Time!

Yeah, just me and my new future.

As soon as my parents left, I met up with some of the kids I'd met at orientation a couple of weeks ago. I texted everyone and we gathered at the Commons. This kid named Brandon pulled out a blunt, fired it up right there in broad daylight, and passed it around. We all started smoking and soon we were flying. Everyone had a story about how glad they were to make their escape and be here in the land of the free.

The group of us, which was me, Brandon, Doudji, and a few others decided to take a walk around. Doudji was a dude from Haiti, and he was my first roommate. I thought he was pretty cool because he had that French and Creole accent, and he looked like he knew which end was up. My first impression was that he and I would become close friends, but after I lived with him for a while I couldn't believe what a slob he was. I've never met someone smellier and dirtier than Doudji. He was a great friend, and down to earth, but Jesus, he stunk! He was just not my type of person to hang out with.

Of course I didn't know it at the time, but Brandon would be my next roommate, and become my ride or die, best friend, drug partner, and friend for life. Brandon was this dude from Philadelphia, and he looked like a typical Philly goon with a crazy long beard and something about him that made him look like a schemer. Little did I know Brandon would do anything for me and go to any length to look out for me. It turns out that Brandon was a Capricorn just like me, so we had this strong astrological connection...we thought about stuff the same way, we both liked to keep our rooms clean and straight (so there was no shit lying around in case of a bust), and it was like we knew what each other was thinking without having to say it. Yo, Brandon!

The group of us was pretty stoned, and we were in a good head space looking for some fun so we decided to go to the mall, to the Providence Place Mall, to check it out and do a little shopping.

So here it is, my first day of freedom, and guess who I saw in the mall? I met Hermione from Harry Potter. It was Emma Watson! Emma was going to Brown, and she was doing a little school shopping with her mom.

So I went up to her, said hi, and introduced myself, and she was real nice, and smiled. She had good energy.

So while I'm telling her how great it is to meet her, some college girls come by and they start yelling, "Hermione! Hermione!" like screaming it, and her mom turns around, and yells, "Shut the fuck up! Shut the fuck up! Her name is not Hermione, you assholes, her name is Emma!" It was just a little funny. Yeah, so Emma laughed and the girls shut up and we all went on our way.

The mall was kind of cool, lots of great shops, and we got some snacks at the food court; I saw some Air Jordans I liked, and we all carried on, shooting the shit, freewheeling and laughing. Everything felt so good! I had my eyes out for the ladies because everywhere I looked there were these beautiful sexy women, and I knew I had to get some.

After that we're back in the dorms, and I decided to roam around and meet people. So I went knocking on doors, wandering from door to door and floor to floor introducing myself. This is like the best thing you can do, and it's weird that hardly anybody does it. Most good things that come to you in life come through people, not birds or rocks or tables or carpeting! You know? Think about it. It's only by meeting people that you get the juice flowing. Most people are nice, and they're glad you went out of your way to say hi. Sure, there'll be a few losers who will turn Mr. Grumpy on you, but that's the 1% crowd and you don't want to know them anyway. My advice is be bold, smile, show your teeth, and get around. You never know what you'll find, and most often you'll be amazed. Later you'll see how this works out for me.

So that afternoon with a new buzz on, I got to meet a lot of the people living in the rooms around me, and I got to shake the hands of dozens of nice-looking ladies. I remember their nicely shaped mouths, cute laughter, fragrant perfumes, and they all wore warm smiles for me. This was going to be great!

Later on I'm walking out of the dorm to go to the store, and two dudes are walking by in the lobby. Something happens and they drop all their stuff on the floor, so I'm helping them pick it all up and we're laughing about it, and this is how I met my good friends Nick and Neil. They invite me to go upstairs with them, so I go upstairs to their room and they have a freezer full of booze! They've got all kinds of vodka, chasers, mixes, and it was awesome! They poured me a shot and we sat down to talk, and then they opened up a safe. Inside was a massive amount of marijuana. I'm like, wow! These are the kids I need to hang out with!

I know we met for a reason so from there we just sort of all got ready to go out for the night. We drank some more vodka and smoked a few numbers and began to get really wasted.

Nick and Neil are actually from Rhode Island, which was kind of surprising. Most of the JW kids I had met today were from out of state. So here I am with two natives. Neil was like the muscle, a little short Guido, you know what I mean? He was jacked up, with ripped muscles and slicked back hair. He looked like somebody you'd want to keep your eye on. Nick was just the opposite; he was a little skinny short guy just like me, and a fast talker, you know, also like me, but you knew he was the moneymaker, the schemer, the crafty little son of a bitch you'd better watch out for. So, you know, what am I doing with these two kids, man?

So we were fucking hammered. Shots of vodka, smoking heavy duty shit for an hour or more… I lost track of time…and now we have a couple of other kids with us. Christy, Airica, Andrew, and Doudjy joined us and we went out to Federal Hill which is one of Providence's hottest clubbing areas. Of course we're all underage but that doesn't matter. Nick and Neil were locals and they knew everybody, so they got us straight in without IDs.

We hit it hard! We get into the club, the music is blasting, there are all these beautiful chicks on the dance floor, the booze is flowing, and everybody is having a great time! The music was loud and wild, the bass beating out the rhythm. They've got rotating green, red, and yellow floodlights highlighting the dancers, and strobe lights flashing. Everybody was celebrating, hands in the air, and the smell of booze, perfume and sex was in my nose. Yeah, man!

So we laid it down. We were ordering shots left and right, and everybody was buying, and I swear we dropped about $15,000 that night! Nick and Neil spent five Gs apiece because they were buying shots for our group and all the girls that came by our table, and buying expensive bottles, and we had the best seating. We got pretty rowdy and got kicked out of a couple of bars, you know? We were just going at it, kids out of high school dropping heavy cash and blowing it out because this was our freedom night. And there comes a point where you don't give a damn anymore; it was like whatever. So on our first night out we just killed it.

It's like 2 o'clock in the morning and we're hammered, and our crew is back in the street, walking to the dorms. Me and Nick got lost, so this is like our time to really get close. We're walking back, and I mean we are just so drunk we're walking on the highway. We're just really fucked up, man, and we're destroying stuff along the way, just fucking shit up in Providence, knocking shit over, being reckless kids starting college. So that's how Nick and I got started.

The next morning we wake up with a banging headache and now we have to go to the inauguration speech. The inauguration speech was to welcome all the students to the new school year. It was also a ceremony for the graduates of the year before, and as I'm sitting there, I meet these two girls next to me. These two girls start talking to me and Doudjy, and they want to hang out after. So I'm down with that. I'm always down for everything! One girl was Shelby and the other was

Johanna. Shelby was a gorgeous Dominican mami from Washington Heights, and she looked exactly like Asia. What a beauty!

Johanna would later become one of my main fuck buddies, but now me and Shelby were hitting it off. Shelby had curly black hair, a nice rack, and she was coming on to me. I could tell she was going to be number one! After the ceremony was over I took her back to the dorm room and got my first piece of college ass, laid on the second day. Man, she was good! We enjoyed each other most of the afternoon.

After that, Shelby took me shopping. Earlier she had said to me, "Yeah, like if you're good in bed, I'll take you shopping." She was a little rich girl, so I said I'm okay with that, cool, whatever. So after I'd balled the crap out of her, we went shopping and had a good time. I guess I did good! Screwing Shelby went on for a few months... Until she saw how much I got around.

Back at the dorm we said goodbye and I wound up running into her friend, Johanna, who I met at the ceremony. Now Johanna starts coming on to me as well... so guess what? It didn't take much to chat her up and get her into bed, and I had them both on the same day! A few months later this came out and there was trouble between the two girls because they both wanted me between their sheets.

So it's the first day of classes. I'm excited! I walk into my classrooms, and it was, you know, just very crazy, new people, new faces, all this intense energy...the rooms smelled fresh, there were girls from all around the world, and it was an overall class of cool-ass kids. I met kids that day who will always be my best friends. It was like, wow, just an amazing time. It's like not only was I a million miles from home, screwing new chicks, getting wasted and partying all the time, but it was also that there was so much to choose from! It was like being a chocoholic in a cocoa factory.

I wound up meeting the craziest girl who ever went to Johnson & Wales. Her name was Sherry and she was from Connecticut. The crazy thing about her was she ate her own hair. She would pull her hair out and then eat it. She had a lot of crazy issues going on in her life, and was a stalkerish type of girl. She also had a tail. This was the first girl I met in my classes. I also met my four friends, Devin, Josh, Drew and Matt, whose name is Philly. It didn't take long for us to get close, and now the year was really kicking off.

Chapter 4

Setting the Pace

College life quickly became a bunch of parties. Schoolwork took a backseat and pretty much every weekend we'd go out. We'd go to Finnegan's Wake Draft House on Fridays. Finnegan's is an Irish pub and it's in downtown Providence. They had good Irish whiskey and Guinness, nice dark, tall glasses of Guinness. We'd also go to Ultra the Night Club on Thursdays which was a very popular club. Pauly D spins there a lot, and I met Pauly D on the week before the Jersey Shore aired in 2009. There were all kinds of wild and crazy women there, and the action was hot. We would go to Jerky's Bar on Richmond on Wednesday nights. It was a little dive bar for underage drinking college kids. I heard they're closed now.

It's about the third week of school and I get into an argument with my friends Nick and Neil. We had all gone out the night before, and they decided to go to a club called Therapy. It was open almost all night and it's like a rave club, with a lot of ecstasy and other drugs, and a lot of horny women. I decided to stay in and pass on that night's fun. A man's got to earn a living and by this time I was selling massive amounts of weed, about two or three kilos a week to dozens of college kids. But then what happened is we wound up getting a shitty batch of weed. Fuck!

I didn't want to get stuck with it so I told Neil to take it and soak it in rum, spray it on top with a strawberry scent from the smoke shop, and this is how we were going to turn it into Jamaican rum kush, strawberry rum kush. So Neil says he'll do this, and he took the shit. I went back to my room, got loaded, and passed out. I must've had a blackout, because I don't remember anything. Neil was supposed to have the stuff back in my room, but I woke up in the morning and forgot that he had returned the kush, and I had stashed it so nobody could find it if there was a raid on the room. So I'm looking for it and I can't find it. Now I'm thinking like Neil and Nick ripped me off. So I go down to their room and I drag them out of bed. I was really pissed because I'd already been ripped off once.

Mind you, these are my best friends in college so far, you know, the first three weeks, and I'm arguing with them, and I'm ready to fight, and it's like whatever, whatever, whatever, and I wind up going back to my room empty-handed, totally hung over, insulted, and fucking pissed off...only to find the stash later. Thank you, Jesus! Like a dummy, I'd hidden the kush in a place where even I almost didn't find it! So I told Neil, "Neil, listen, I found it." He didn't care and said, "Whatever, man." After all that piss and vinegar, he could just let it go as easily as that. That's why I love these guys.

Another interesting story about Neil was our first brawl. This was one of several and it shows how wild we were. So it was almost October and I was with Airica; we were getting it on and the stroking was sweet. I heard later that Neil was in Alex's room and he was tapping her ass and riding her with pleasure, too. All of a sudden we both got a text from Chowder, saying that he got jumped walking back from Jerky's Bar. We both literally hop up in mid-stroke and rush out into the hall half naked. Throwing on the rest of our clothes, we ran out of the dorms as fast as we could and started searching for Chowder.

We ran about a quarter mile down the road and couldn't find Chowder; we were about to turn back, but then we rounded a corner by the Sovereign Bank and Starbucks and there in the street was Trotta and a whole bunch of angry kids. Chowder was Nick's roommate and friends with Neil, and we rushed to Chowder's side. That's when the brawl began. Remember that Neil is this Italian Guido the size of Ronnie from Jersey Shore, and Chowder is even bigger. We jumped into the middle and each of us picked one dude apiece and started scrapping! We were throwing punches and kicks, and I landed my fist square on the nose of this big ugly looking white boy. I heard a snap and saw the blood coming out of his nose. Trotta was throwing punches and he had worked his assailant backwards a few feet; Neil was hitting this tall dude with steel fists, and the dude was bleeding from his cheek.

At that point, the two guys Chowder and I were fighting pulled back and ran down the street so I swung around to help Neil and the two of us demolished him. By this time he was on the ground and he was just getting punished and his girlfriend begged us to please stop... And since the fight was over, we did. Neil and I got off the dude, and he was getting up really slowly, his girlfriend wiping his bloody face. We asked Trotta what was going on and he said he was selling them some weed, and things got out of hand. I thought it was probably because he made a pass at one of the girls. Whatever. We got Chowder in the car and went back to the dorms. Neil and I went back up to the girls' rooms to finish what we started, but they had enough of our pipe-laying for Wednesday night... So there was no more of that. Shit. But it's okay. (You're welcome, Trotta.)

So the next day I see Neil, Nick and Chowder. Chowder's on his way out the door along with Neil and Nick, so I asked him where everybody's going. These three dudes were all suited up and they're going to an interview. An interview? Shit, I want to go, too! I didn't even know where they were going.

I said screw it. Hell, I was dressed well enough, so we all get into the car and drive over to this fraternity. So I'm like, hell, what's this all about? I never really knew much about fraternities and pledging and stuff like that. I'd heard about it, and I knew JWU had a bunch of them, but I never really thought much about it.

We pull up to the Zeta Beta Tau fraternity house. It's the world's first Jewish fraternity. I'm thinking WTF? You guys are interested in joining a fraternity? Why would you want to do that?

We park the car and go in the front door of this big house. Two of the ZBT brothers greet us at the door and ask us if we've come to be interviewed. We say sure, so we're led into the house and we're told to sit down, have a Coke, and wait our turn. Some of the brothers came up to us and asked our names and a few other questions like where do we live, why are we interested in ZBT and shit like that.

We wound up going through the interview process. Each of us got called into the basement one by one, and it's the weirdest thing. I was totally not expecting this. They did this weird shit to us, like having to hold a brick in each hand as they asked us questions while shining this bright light in our eyes. The questions were reckless, like if you saw a big titted blonde girl at the bar and she was hot for you but one of your brothers is getting jumped outside, what would you do? Shit! I know what I'd do! What would YOU do?

Another question was about making a deal for a case of beer and paying less than you were supposed to, would you pocket the difference or take the extra back to your brothers? These questions pissed me off! I was like I'm going to fuck this guy up! Plus I didn't like holding the fucking bricks! And I didn't like the light in my eyes!

But it was kind of an interesting experience. It was all new to me, interviewing for a fraternity. So the four of us finished the interviews, and then we were told to go home, and we'd be contacted about our bids. The way it works is you go to the fraternity you want to pledge to, get interviewed like we did, and then the house will contact you and tell you if they will offer you a bid to pledge with them. Not all fraternities or sororities will want to recruit you, for whatever reason, so if you really have your heart set on joining a Greek, you could be pretty upset if you don't get a bid. ZBT was an outlaw fraternity, meaning they weren't sanctioned by the university, but that only made them seem even more interesting to me!

Okay, so we had to wait a week or so to see if we'd get our bid, and finally bid night acceptance is rolling around. We got word to return to ZBT, but that didn't mean that we were going to get a bid, because sometimes they tell you to come to the house just to see how disappointed you are. So anyway, we went to the house and when we got there it was like: everybody meet the fuck outside. So they made it feel dangerous by meeting with us under a bridge. It was dark and creepy and we were down there under the bridge with all this trash, broken fencing, high weeds, and traffic going by overhead.

They split us up, me, Nick, Neil, and Chowder. We were all best friends, and we're all tight and everything, and the frat boys called us The Four Goonies. They split us up into different cars, and we get to this old house that was in shambles. We were blindfolded and taken into the house, made to walk up and down stairs, and they walked us around through the rooms which stunk of stale piss and vomit. We were told to take off our blindfolds, and then we saw everyone around who had received bids to join ZBT. There were about 20 of us. This was my pledge class.

This is when Cheese and I got to know each other better. His real name was Quis but everybody called him Cheese. He was a pledge brother and one of the cheapest bastards you ever met. I'd seen him on the basketball courts the first week or two of school, so I kind of knew him. This is when I also met Milhem. I'd seen him around before because we'd both had sex with a lot of girls. I'd heard he had a threesome with some girls, so he and I had a high regard for each other, you know what I mean? We all connected, and I thought, "Wow! This is going to be awesome!"

So now we're pushing around Halloween and this is when I wind up getting into my first bit of trouble in college. This is a pretty interesting story. My history is that I've never ever had a good Halloween. Something bad always happens, like I wake up in the hospital or get into fights, or whatever. Something bad always happens. It's crazy. This Halloween was no different.

I was going to a party with my girls. It was me, Erica, Alex, Carlin, Lexi and Jamie Jones. Brandon and Doudji were with me, too. We were totally high but in a good place, you know? The girls were chatting about school, and guys they liked, and shit they'd bought, so the energy was light and fun. Man, I love the sound of women's laughter; there's nothing like it. Sexy and playful; just the thing to bring the man out in me.

Since there are a lot of us, we take a van and a taxi to get to where we're going, and we step out of the vehicles. I was paying for the ride because drug sales were going through the roof; I was selling more than a kilo a day and was now also handling all kinds of pills. Business was great and I didn't carry cash; all I had was a credit card. So I'm, like, using my credit card. Here it is, ring us up and we'll be all set to go. The driver says to me, in a real angry tone, "We don't take credit cards." And then he said, "Fuck you" to me in Spanish and called me a bitch ass bag. "All of you! Get back in the cab!" he ordered. "I'm going to drop you back off where I picked you up. You can fucking walk back here." So I said, "Alright, cool."

He takes us back to where we started. The girls are quiet; they're all bummed out. Our evening has turned to shit because of this stupid asshole. We get out of the car and I knocked the guy the fuck out. Bam! Bam! Bam! This motherfucker is on the ground with a bloody mouth.

But there's a group of taxi drivers waiting on the wall, this bastard's friends, and they all jump into the fight, so now it's a three-on-ten brawl. Me, Brandon and Doudji versus these 10 taxi drivers. We beat the living shit out of them.

Okay, so now the cops come. One of the drivers had called them, and they snatch me up. I had a NY Yankee ball cap on my head, and my roommates had on silly hats and Boston hats, so the cops told them they could go, but they kept me. They told me us New Yorkers were fucking up New England, and they were going to teach me what they do to NY fuck-ups like me. So they put me in cuffs and threw me in the squad car.

When the cop had me in the car, I could see that this cop's name was Corporal Robinson. So I said like, "Well, Dude, like, you know what I mean? Like, bro, we both have the same last names. Cut me some slack." The cop said, "Fuck you." So that was going nowhere.

Now the chief comes over to the squad car. He says, "Hey, what was that in this turd's hands?" The cop replies, "He had a little Gatorade bottle full of vodka." So the chief says, "Okay, give me that," and he chugged down the bottle in front of me and then told the cop, "Do whatever you gotta do with him."

So the cop is driving me around, and whatever, and I told him he should pull onto a side street. "You and me," I said. "Let's fight one-on-one and if I beat the shit out of you, you let me go. If you win, you take me to jail." Well, the cop was too chicken shit to say yes, and he wouldn't do it. So we get to the jail, and he books me. After processing, which took forever, I was allowed my one phone call, which was home to my lawyer. I got right out of there. As soon as I got out of the jail, I went back to the dorms, and I was thinking that my friends had left me at the brawl. That's how hammered I was, and that's why I don't like Halloween.

I was worried about getting kicked out of school. Because of the taxicab brawl, and my getting singled out by the PPD, I have to go to my first conduct meeting. A conduct meeting is like a student disciplinary hearing where the incident is described to school officials and you have the opportunity to tell your side of the story. Then the officials think about it and decide if they should kick your ass home, or if the tuition you're paying is more important.

To tell the truth, they should have kicked my ass home. It was only two months into the year and I was doing reckless shit all around the city.

The good news is that the taxi driver never showed up at the conduct meeting. He was either sober now, or was too scared to see me again, or he needed to pay the bills and keep the babies fed. We've all got our problems, you know?

So I get off Scot free. The day I get out of trouble I'm with my buddy Brandon. Brandon was one of my bros that the cops let go in the taxicab incident. I get out of the conduct meeting that morning and Brandon and I are going to find some ladies to go out with us and celebrate. Along the way we find my buddy, Kyle. We decide we're going to raise the roof at Finnegan's, but we run into a going-away party in the dorms for this cute girl, Danielle. So we step into the dorm party…and they've got more shit going on here than in Finnegan's!

There were about 150 Jello shots, three pints of vodka, three handles of whiskey, pitchers, bottles, all types of drugs in the room, Captain Morgan, and enough alcohol to knock out a room full of sailors. Just as soon as the door closes behind us, the Resident Advisor starts knocking on the door.

Holy shit, I can't catch a break. I just got out of conduct...now I have to go back in!

So the room is raided and everyone is stashing their drugs, and there is this one psycho crazy moment as this room full of kids is going ape shit. Everyone has their name listed and everyone is in serious trouble.

But me and Brandon wind up getting off because everybody there kept saying that Vic and Brandon had just walked into the room. I mean, we weren't even dressed to go out or anything. We didn't even have a single drink. So the RAs wound up letting us go. And even though we still had to go to conduct to explain what we were doing there, we got off. That was my second time at a disciplinary hearing...and it wasn't my last.

Funny thing about Turbs. He was the kid that lived across the hall from me. Turbs broke out of the room and was running down the hallway. Before he got to the exit stairs, the RA yelled at him to come back. As the stairwell door was closing, we could all hear Turbs yelling back at the RA, "Fuck you! Catch me in the line at Finnegan's!" and the RA was really pissed off.

CHAPTER 4

The Bitch Ass Pussies of Delta Upsilon

So it was the end of the first trimester and Thanksgiving break was right about then. There was no point staying at school, and Mom and Dad wanted me home, so I went back to Pennsylvania for Thanksgiving. But my life wasn't there anymore and I was missing my college family. I hated being home because it was only more of all the things and reasons I had left.

I found myself counting the days, and counting the hours until I could be back on the bus headed north. Yes, there was Thanksgiving dinner, and mom's cooking was as good as always, but it was then that I realized that Pa had nothing else to offer me. And though that was sad, because even though I was running away from them and toward my destiny, I really did love them both. When you take a moment and breathe in slowly, thinking about where you've come from and where you're going, there is that feeling in your heart that's both sweet and bitter when you know you're too big for the nest and have to make your own way from now on. The last minute of the last hour of the last day finally came and it was a relief to be on that bus.

Now we're rolling into Christmas time. It was cold and there was snow on the ground, all the stores were lit up with Christmas lights and everything was ring-ting-tingaling. The money tree was still dispensing loads of cash from all the drug sales coming out of my room, and it was crazy! We were selling weed, E-pills, uppers, downers, just about any kind of prescription drug you could think of. We were moving a lot of shit. The money was flowing in and it was going to be a merry Christmas.

On December 17, 2009, we're sitting inside the dorms, just as high as hell, bored out of our skulls, me, Nick, Neil, Brandon, and Chowder. I was high on some shit, and just bored, plain old stupid-ass bored.

So I've got the window open and I'm screaming out the window at another fraternity, Delta Upsilon. There were some Delta Upsilons on the path below my window and I yelled out the window at them, "Hey, look at the bitch ass pussies!" And I'm just screaming at them, screaming at them, screaming at them. Pretty screwy, right? But I wasn't in my right mind anyway, after all the drugs, alcohol, sex and attitude I'd been getting away with. Shit! I was a drug king. If I wasn't getting high or getting laid, I needed some other kind of entertainment and action.

So now they're the ones that are yelling back, defending their pride, and they want to fight! So Neil storms outside. I go with Neil to raise hell, and when we get outside, the Deltas aren't even there! Neil and I have our blood up, and we're pissed, and we're looking for a fight, but there's no one to fight so we head back into the dorms and go back to our room.

Up in our room we're hanging out, and now the Deltas come back talking shit. We run out there again but this time I was smart, and I went upstairs to change my clothes first, and then I went outside so the cameras couldn't tell it was me. We get outside, and there were like 30 fraternity kids there. They had gone back to their house to bring a small army! When I got out there, Neil's in between them talking shit, and they're all scared of Neil. When he powers up, you don't want to be standing in front of him. It turns out that the biggest Delta Upsilon kid in the group, a 6-foot-3 three hundred pound Asian kid comes at Neil. Neil slams him on the ground and then the brawl started. Neil is yelling, "Don't hit him! Don't hit him!" But I come up and hit him in the face anyway. The kid's shoulder is dislocated, and a kid to the side of him is coming at me and is about to knock me out when my buddy Chowder knocked him out instead, I mean Chowder just clinked him. It was bad and he broke the kid's nose. So now everything is scattered with kids running all over the place, some girls are screaming, and it wasn't long before the RAs showed up.

It was five on 30. We beat the shit out of these kids. It was the biggest brawl at Johnson & Wales since 2003. We were brutal and left them with broken noses and pummeled faces; we saw that crowd limping home. Oh, shit! This was now going to be my third conduct meeting.

And the funny thing was that my dorm room neighbor, Arez, had just been pledged into the Delta Upsilon fraternity. I go next door to see Andrew and I'm telling him, "Like, Dude, listen, don't say anything," you know? I get upstairs and now there's cops and everything. Neil, Chowder, Brandon and Nick left but I stayed. I'm walking around the dorm and the kids that are there are saying, "It was you! It was you!" and I said, "I didn't do anything. I'm still here. If it was me, I would've run away."

It didn't matter because the next day Chowder told security everything, he told them the truth. So I'm thinking, "Screw it. I'm not going to tell my parents anything. I'm going to go home for Christmas and come back."

Well, Christmas was not going to be quite so merry. The five of us were going home for Christmas not knowing if it we're going to be allowed to come back. We didn't know if we should tell our parents that we were getting kicked out, or just keep quiet and see what happened in the New Year. It sure put a damper on our holiday season. All of us were unsettled.

Now it's the new year and we get back from Christmas. We start pledging. I'm in the room drinking, getting ready for Brandon's birthday, and I'm hammered again and the guys say we have to go to the ZBT house because it's pledging time.

We started pledging with 14 kids, and crossed with only four. 78% of my group never made it through. Pledging was six weeks long with three days each week for pledging activities, and our fraternity was off campus. Zeta Beta Tau was made up of a bunch of goons, a bunch of reckless goon juice heads from New York and from everywhere around New York City. And this crowd was just ready to fuck shit up. And we wound up pledging to this insane fraternity! The first night of pledge it was so crazy that the biggest kid in our group, whose name was Matt Role, he just up and ran out of the building and then dropped out of school... How nuts is that?

The fraternity brothers had told us to be at the house at 9 o'clock. We got into Nick Jones car, and since there were 14 of us, we also used Brandon's blue car, and somebody else had a car. Teddy drove his pickup truck. We're on the road and wound up breaking down in a big snow storm. The car wouldn't start and we finally wound up getting to the house around 11:45 p.m. The brothers beat the shit out of us for being late, and told us to go into the hallway to talk it over and see if we really wanted to go through with our pledging. So we go into the hall, and we all decided yeah, because we were crazy motherfuckers, and now it's time to decide who's going to be first in line to get fucked up.

So of course I'm number one in line. Neil didn't want to go first, so I'm first and they put my name on my shirt and led me up to the attic in the pitch black dark. I get up to the attic and the brothers up there were just crazy! They had gas masks on, and were walking around you, creeping in your face; I'm on my knees with my head down, and there were holes in the attic floor, and it was nuts.

The rest of the pledges are brought up there, and we were all scared because of the shit that was going on and I was so drunk I really can't tell you much about the first night. But I can tell you it was very intense. There was a lot of talk and meeting everyone... And we wind up getting back to the dorm around 6 a.m. It was one fucking night to remember, and I wish I did.

With that first pledge night over, now comes my third conduct meeting. The day I get the letter from the conduct committee, we're all on a scavenger hunt for the fraternity. We all told Neil not to go home so he wouldn't miss the conduct meeting, but you can't tell Neil what he doesn't want to hear and he wasn't going to listen. He left school and headed back home.

We needed witnesses stating that we weren't involved in the Delta Upsilon brawl, and we had Josh M and Matt, aka Philly. I chose Matt and everybody's laughing at me. "Why'd you choose Matt?" they asked. "He's kind of dumb!" I chose Matt because even though he seemed like a dumb kid, I knew he knew. I knew he was smarter than he seemed, smarter than he came off to be. That's why I took Philly. Brandon took Josh. And Chowder was there with Nick's dad...who just happened to be the president architect of the whole fucking school.

So the day came for the conduct meeting, and it wound up being eight hours long. It's a formal hearing and one by one we all tell our stories, and bring in our witnesses to back ourselves up. When it's my turn, I told the story I wanted the officials to hear, and I brought in my witness, Matt. The officer in charge of the meeting asked Matt what he knew about the brawl, and Matt told him, "Vic was out there with me, and he got a girl's number, but he was just watching the fight. He was not involved. I was with Vic the whole time," so he did good by backing me up.

In his closing statement, Matt said, "Vic is a good kid! Everyone loves him, all the ladies love him, and if you kick Vic out, we're going to cause a ruckus at this school!"

Now it's time for my dorm room neighbor, Arez, to come in and tell his story. Like I said, Arez was in the Delta Upsilon fraternity, he had just got in, and these are his new fraternity brothers...but he knew me through orientation, and we had a lot of classes together, and we lived right next door to each other, along with Brandon, Chowder, Nick and Neil. The pressure on him was intense because on the one hand he's expected to be loyal to his new fraternity brothers, and on the other hand we're his buddies from the dorm.

Arez comes into the hearing room, and he starts shaking like Cassius Clay. I'm staring at him hard because the night before the conduct meeting I went to his room and I told him, "If you tell anyone what really happened, I'm going to beat the shit out of you!" You know, just scaring him a little. Brandon warned me not to do that, but I told Brandon to shut the fuck up. I knew what I was doing.

So we're in the conduct meeting and Arez walks in. He looked at all of us and then he started shaking and crying, and he needed water. The conduct lady across from me looks at me and she's telegraphing me with her smile that she knows I'm full of shit and I'm going down. I can see in her smile and eyes that she's thinking, "Ha! We got this!", but I'm thinking there's more to this than meets the eye, so I wait for Andrew to tell his story, and he says, "Like, you know, you guys are my fraternity brothers, but these kids are my best friends." Arez pointed at me and said, "That kid, right there, he's my best friend in this room, and he would never, ever, do anything to harm anyone!" I said out loud, "Point well taken!"

His fraternity brothers look at him, and they're really ticked off because Arez isn't helping and they were sure they had me! They said they couldn't identify any of the kids in the conduct meeting. The only kid they could recognize wasn't there, and that was Neil.

So they asked the conduct officers if they could get Neil on the phone. The conduct officers get Neil on the phone, and Neil says, "What? Fuck all of this shit! Fuck Johnson & Wales, and fuck all of you! I'll fuck up all your shit! I did everything! I fucked those kids up, and I fuck your school and fuck your dorm, and fuck your rules, and fuck your…" and he just went off, and they pretty much gave him the boot from school right there.

I just walked away Scot free again. But it was funny, you know what I mean? On my way into the conduct meeting, I took care of the situation the way you're supposed to. I dressed for the part and had my glasses on so I'd look a little wimpy, and I was dressed conservatively, held my suit jacket over my arm, and looked like a good college kid. I was ready to go. And I already knew who said what, and knew how to get around all their personalities. I had scoped everything and stacked the deck in my favor and I knew I would totally blow through all that shit. It was literally me and Brandon against everyone in that room. So it was sweet, really sweet, when I got away with everything. I'd been here three times now. And that was that. I never told my parents what the fuck had gone on until after graduation over three years later.

Chapter 5

Pledging with the Zeta Beta Tau Maniacs

Now it's around February and we're getting deeper into pledging. It began to get very intense because the ZBT brothers wanted to weed out the weaker pledges so only the best would remain and cross into the fraternity. Because it got so intense and was getting a bit outrageous, a lot of the kids in my pledge group began to drop out.

The ZBT pledges were going through hell, getting beaten up with all kinds of difficult tasks. There were heavy workouts, and weird workouts, too, like getting into a push-up position, but on our elbows, and forced to stay that way for five minutes, often while a fraternity brother was yelling profanities in our ears.

Another time we had to rub tiger balm on our balls and do calisthenics. We had to jump and run in place, and kick our legs high, and all the while our balls were on fire! Then we had to run up to the third floor of the house and back down again as the brothers were bashing us with pillows, knocking us down, screaming at us and laughing their asses off. It was a brutal morning, trust me.

And then there was the drinking. There was a lot of that! It was common to be told to drink 10 beers in 30 minutes. We didn't get drunk because the carbonation in our bellies made us throw up. And, of course, you'd have to walk down a gauntlet of brothers as they punched you on your arm in the same spot. Oh, yeah, one time our sister sorority tried to kidnap us. It was an outrageous event; they were waiting for us at the corner in a blue car. Our pledge master warned us and told us to watch out for the blue car, so we thought it was detectives or something. We were coming back with loads of food for the brothers, and the sisters just went off! We wound up getting away, but they stole our phones, and the brothers went back and poured paint on one of their cars…it was crazy. Through all of this shit, we weren't allowed to cut or wash our hair, so all of us began to have long matted hair with itchy scalps. There was a lot of psychological abuse, and the pledges were always kept in a fearful mode, nervous 24/7, never knowing what was coming next.

From my group of friends, Cheese dropped, Milhem dropped, Chowder was a pussy and had to go home every weekend, Neil never showed up…and one by one the rest of the kids in my pledge group all dropped out. One day it wound up being just me.

I had made it far enough along to when it was time to choose my big brother in the fraternity. One of the brothers named Billy pulled me aside and we sat down to talk. Billy said, "Vic, I want you to be my little brother." I was, all right! Let's get this done! Billy was one of the cool brothers and I knew he would set me up and watch my back. I was all pumped about it.

The next day was the day we were going to get our big brother assignments. So the few pledges that were left were blindfolded and taken upstairs. When we got there, the big brothers were going to give their speech about the pledges and why they're choosing one or the other of us. I'm number one to be assigned, so I'm expecting to hear Billy's voice, but I don't! It's somebody else. It was shocking! I wind up getting Mikey Mojo and I didn't know who the hell Mojo was. I hear Mojo's voice and it was like, wow, man, who the hell is this guy?

It turned out that getting Moj as my big brother was the best thing that could have happened, you know? Mojo took care of everybody, like he treated everybody like they were his little brother. Whatever you needed, you could see Moj and tell him, and he'd help you out. He's a great guy, and even to this day I hit up Mojo when I need some advice or a quick zap of positive energy. Anything I need, anything, that's my family. It was Moj who named me The Black Irish, you know?

After the assignments were made, everybody was celebrating and they gave me a bottle of vodka and we're all getting drunk. I get hammered, and the party goes until almost dawn, until you can see the night clouds with just the beginning of morning light on them. When I woke up, I was still at the fraternity house, and I'd thrown up all over myself, man. I was all screwed up, and I'm thinking, holy shit, I have this huge midterm today! But I'm so fucking drunk, I can barely crawl my way to the front door. I woke up one of my brothers and he said, "Find Luke! He's going that way now." I had to get inside the classroom by 9:30 or they would lock the doors and I'd miss the test.

I had to gun it down there! I look at the clock and I can barely make out the numbers to tell what time it is because my vision is blurry and my brain is foggy. I have enough of my wits to realize I have to hurry to get to class, but I'm reeking of alcohol, smelling of puke and God knows what, and I still have my pledge clothes on. To help me wake up I jumped into the shower, threw some hot water on me, changed my clothes and got a ride downtown with Luke. I barely get to class on time and fall into my seat. My ex-fling, Kate Jabs, and my buddy, Corey, are sitting next to me. Corey knows I'm pledging, and he knows what it's like because he just finished pledging. And he says to me, "You know what, man? Go home. Go back to the dorms and I'll do the whole motherfucking test for you." Holy shit! An angel from heaven! Corey took my midterm for me, and I got a 90 on it. I went back to the dorms and finally got some sleep. I was beat.

Aside from all the hazing, we also went on a bunch of scavenger hunts. They were fun, but they were outrageous and risky. One of the things we had to do was get street signs as souvenirs for the fraternity, and we had to pull down these street signs at 6:00 a.m. in front of all the morning traffic! One of the street signs we had to collect was the Francis Street sign in

Providence, which is the main road going to the freeway and the mall. We almost got arrested doing that. We had just finished tearing down the sign when a squad car came up. They were blocked by traffic but the cop used his loudspeaker and told us to freeze. Hell, we didn't freeze! We grabbed the sign and jumped into our car and then we were chased by the cops. The jammed-up morning traffic helped us and we dodged left on one street, right on the other, and slipped inside an alley. It was pretty hectic, but we got away.

Another time we stole an Italian flag from a flagpole in downtown Providence, and the cops chased us again. One of my brothers was driving, and he had a bunch of cocaine on him. The cops pulled us over, but we had stuffed everything away...and they figured they had the wrong car and let us go. That was a riot! Very edgy stuff...

There were other fun things to do when we were pledging. One time we had to do a scavenger hunt in Boston, so we headed out on the highway. We had to get pictures with a bunch of strippers, and we had to take nude pictures of each other in the middle of the street, walking around. We had to strip glass bricks out of a building with an ax at midnight with nobody around. We had to get a picture of one of us standing on a cop's car giving the finger, which Milla gleefully did; the cop was in a store and he came barreling out of there chasing us and we all scattered and ran! We also had to take a video of the pledges piggy-back racing on fat girls, and chew gum that we found on bus seats. Yeah.

On another occasion we had to shave our balls and bake the hair into a chocolate cake, which we offered to strangers. We slept in a basement with rats, mice, everything. We had a Concoction Night, which was when the brothers gave the pledges a big pot of stew with all kinds of crap in it including maggots, old moldy food, the brothers' used socks and other nasty things. The fraternity house was so disgusting... There were rats running around, holes in the ceiling, broken windows, stairs that gave under your weight, cobwebs, smelly old curtains, and the stench of old urine and puke. The house was located at 50 Ring Street. This was the house I pledged in.

In spite of all the crap the ZBT brothers put us through, the best part of pledging was building that brotherhood; these were the kids that stood by you through all of the hell.

Cross Night was coming, which is the night you officially join the fraternity as a brother. The night before I crossed, my buddy Arjin is having this huge birthday party with a bunch of strippers, but I can't go because I'm supposed to be at the fraternity house. I'm cool, I'm like whatever. I didn't like the idea of missing Arjin's wild party but it was the last night I was pledging and I had to be at the house. I was missing this blowout party, so Arjin, Quinn, and my roommate

Brandon did something really special for me…they made my bathroom and dorm room into the dorm's smoke shack!

The day before Cross Night, I got back from the fraternity house and everything was hooked up. It was about $2,000 worth of shit put in there to really pimp it out, and make it the real dope! I remember coming back to the dorm and my eyes lit up because my room was now the new chill spot. All the games, movies, snacks, weed, everything you needed…we had it all! I had a few words with Brandon about our room becoming the new hangout, because I was worried it would draw too much attention to us, but he didn't listen.

By this time we were selling two to three pounds of weed every day. We were flooding the dorms with weed, and we had to start putting other kids on to draw the heat away from us. Brandon took all of that over because I was so busy with pledging. But Brandon, because he had several kilos of weed, had stashed it around the room, and he wound up getting too high too often. The dorm management started to catch on, and they had their eyes out for him.

When I got back from the fraternity house, there was a lot of stuff going on in our room, and Brandon had all these people in our room, and they're all partying. They had a huge bong, and they called it the Grandpa. It was a big glass motherfucker that was longer than a didgeridoo! It was putting out more smoke than a volcano! There was a whole bunch of reckless stuff going on. The music was too loud, the laughter was too noisy, girls were in their panties, there's liquor and beer spread all around the room, and everybody is totally loaded. So of course, the room wound up getting raided.

What was so crazy was that earlier this morning I had snuck out of the fraternity house to go to the dorm to take a shower. I needed a shower badly because I was pretty stinky. When I got back to my dorm room, Brandon had saved a bag of White Widow marijuana for me to try out. It was some great shit, sure to make my eyeballs pop. I decided I wanted to smoke some before I went back to the house, so I got out our grinder and ground-up some of this shit and rolled a big fat ass joint. After I got stoned, I didn't think about much of anything, and by mistake I left the grinder out on my side of the room. The grinder had that nice sweet sticky aroma, with some dust and ground-up leaves on it.

Later that night I'm at the fraternity house missing Arjin's party while Brandon's at the dorm, and he's getting ready to go to the stripper party, but he forgets his ID. He goes back upstairs and my yes-man next door, which is my neighbor Arez, is throwing a party of his own. Arez was smoking weed in his room with a bunch of people and he didn't even towel his door…he didn't do anything! So there's a huge cloud of smoke coming out of his room and rolling down the hallway.

Of course the RAs think the smell is coming from my room, so they are about to raid our room. Brandon gets a text warning, so he runs in, grabs up about 10 pounds of weed, stuffs it in a duffel bag, and he's grabbing everything he can grab. We had a little hideout spot underneath the desk where we kept all our bowls, papers, and all that kind of stuff, but the RAs came in and they wrecked through our room. The cops were called, and they took over, and it was one giant fucking mess.

Meanwhile, I'm at the house pledging, and I don't know what the fuck is going on. While I'm away, they reset my ID so I couldn't get into any building in the school, I couldn't get back into the dorm, I couldn't do anything. That was cold! Brandon called me at the fraternity house and told my pledge master what was going on, that the cops were looking for me. This is now our fourth time in trouble together…and one of us really has to go. The RAs, the university, the cops had all had enough of our shit. Fuckin' A!

Meanwhile, me and some other pledges were being told to do another crazy task. While the cops are looking for me, I'm down in the fraternity house's basement cutting up stacks and stacks of magazines to get the letters to all the words of the entire ZBT Credo, and pasting them on the basement wall with fricking blue paint! And we only had three hours to do it or we wouldn't cross! Talk about a mind-fucking job. Rusty dull scissors, musty old magazines, the stench of the blue paint in a freaky confined dark room...I thought I'd pass out! But we did it...we got the ZBT Credo up on the wall. Take a look at this and you can see how intense this shit was:

We, the members of Zeta Beta Tau fraternity, believe that the development of the individual as a responsible, mature member of society is the primary goal of the university today.

We believe that fraternity offers to the university community a unique, desirable and successful means of achieving this goal.

In fulfilling the purposes of fraternity, we dedicate ourselves to the principles of:

INTELLECTUAL AWARENESS. Fraternity creates an atmosphere conducive to the expansion of the individual's intellectual horizons, the interchange of ideas within the academic community and the pursuit of scholastic excellence.

SOCIAL RESPONSIBILITY. Fraternity requires the individual to commit himself and accept his responsibility to participate.

INTEGRITY. Fraternity generates a standard of personal integrity – a framework for the individual to maintain honesty, exhibit loyalty and retain a sense of self-discipline.

BROTHERLY LOVE. Fraternity inspires and expresses the interrelation of the individual with his fellows, his pride in the institution and respect for the wisdom of its tradition.

Yeah, fucking crazy, man. And we wound up screwing it up, too! After we were finished with this crap sometime around 4:00 in the morning, it turns out the paint wasn't even blue. It was motherfucking purple! Holy shit. I thought we'd have to do it all over again. Luckily, the brothers didn't care and didn't even bother going into the basement to see if we'd done it. "Yeah, I bet it looks like shit. Good job, Pukes." And this was on top of not sleeping for 48 hours. We'd been on a 48-hour no-sleep marathon. Yeah, man, that was sick.

The next morning I go to the security office to get my ID turned back on. Brandon's in there, arguing and trying to explain this shit away, but it's no good. The security officers gave us the option. "One of you guys has to go," they said. So Brandon and me go into the hallway and we talk. And Brandon said, "Vic, I don't want to be here. I really don't. You're my best friend, so you go ahead, you finish college, and just hit me up in the future. I'll tell them I left the grinder out. This is on me."

Before I could even respond, Brandon ran back into the room and told the bastards that it was all him. So now Brandon's leaving, he's moving out. He took the hit for all the dorm crap we'd been handing out. He was my bro', and it was going to be shit without him. But he had done a righteous thing for me. It was sort of like the Notorious Big and D-Roc story. To this day we're just as tight as we were during freshman year.

Here it is. It's my Cross Night. I crossed the Zeta Beta Tau outlaw fraternity. They're having a big party for all the pledges who made it, and after the ceremony, my brothers take me into a room full of 150 beautiful, horny partying girls! I got branded and paddled, and my hair was just crazy and disgusting and it's as long as possible since I hadn't had a haircut for three months.

And I walk into this cross party with 150 women. It was great! I had one of the best nights of my life!

The next day, after all the drinking, smoking, and sex, I was tired, but I was in that place where I was happy-tired, you know what I mean? And I was just hanging out, enjoying going out to eat with my brothers, hanging out with them, and I was finally one of them. It was a really good feeling.

Now it was time to go on spring break.

Chapter 6

Spring Break in Miami

I'm going to Miami with my two buddies, Corey and Lucas. Corey has an apartment on Sunny Isles Beach, and he's letting us use it for spring break! Holy shit! We've got this great pad in the middle of Sunny Isles Beach, with all the clubs, access to the beach, and all these amazing ladies with hardly any clothes on. You know what the scene is, right? And we're here for seven days. Everything is getting better and better.

It's a funny world because we wind up meeting these two girls who live in the Johnson & Wales dorms with us. It's Beth and Amber, and they're staying in a hotel just down the street from us. Beth is this nice looking brunette with long hair, really shapely body and sweet looking breasts. She's got a knockout smile and she knows how to give the come-on. Her friend, Amber, is also good-looking with red and black hair down to her shoulders and a nice ass.

It didn't take long for Lucas to score with Beth , and so he's screwing her soon after we get to Corey's apartment. The next day both Beth and Amber come to Corey's apartment and we pull out the vodka and beer and we wind up getting hammered. Here we are in this great apartment with warm Miami weather and getting high with these two sexy ladies. So of course it turned into an orgy party.

One thing led to another and me and Amber are hooking up, and Lucas and Beth. Corey's just there, with no lady to smash and he's like doing nothing except being the fifth wheel. Maybe he was hoping for leftovers, I don't know. So it's like, Dude! Get out, you know? But it's his apartment, so... It was awkward but we take the girls and retire to the bathroom where there was this huge shower. Everybody's clothes come off and the four of us jump into the shower with the water running. It's a very long shower, and I'm fucking Amber in one corner and Lucas is fucking Beth in the other. Oh man, that was so great! The water running over our bodies and the four of us fucking each other senseless. I'm watching Lucas fuck Beth and he's watching me fuck Amber. And we were all freaking buzzed! We had the music up nice and loud and as the song changed, we'd switch partners. You know what I mean? That was kind of cool. We were in the shower a long time! Beth and Amber were really good sex partners and we got to hump those babes the entire week. Ah! It was great having these ladies available whenever we were horny, which was all the time. They didn't mind; they were on vacation, too, and they wanted to get some all day and night, just like us.

Soon after we got into town, me, Lucas, and Corey were looking for marijuana but we couldn't find any. We decided to hang out in this one area of South Beach that looked promising, and sure enough we met this guy and he said he's got some leaves. He's got coke and weed, but all we want is the weed. There is this little guy standing behind him and he's telling us not to fuck with the guy we're talking to. "Don't fuck with him, he has fake leaves! Buy from me, I have trees!"

Well, the guy we're dealing with said, "Whatever, whatever, don't listen to him. He's always on my case about some shit." So we walk on with this guy, and I started speaking Creole with him because I'm Haitian. "Yeah, yeah," he says, "I've got some good shit."

We pay $100 and we get the bag of weed. We're walking away and we start smelling it and it smells okay so we said screw the beach, you know, we're going back to Corey's place to smoke. On our way back, we check the bag of weed a little more, and when we dig down, it had shake on top, just a little bit of weed on top to give it the smell, but when we opened it all the way, it was nothing but palm tree leaves. Right in the heart of South Beach, you know what I mean?

Now we go back, and I'm pissed. I'm ready to go fuck this guy up. All we got was this shit. We paid $100, and Corey pulled out his money and bought it before we could even check the fricking bag.

Of course this guy is now long gone, probably in some alley laughing at us. But we saw the other guy, the little guy. And he yelled at us, "I told you, I told you! Come with me."

The little dude takes us down this alley and there's this 7-foot Jamaican dude with dreads. He was like, oh? Now we got a problem with these little motherfuckers? And the little dude said, "No. No, man, no. That dude, Mark, he stole our quarter." So the Jamaican dude says, "Aw, okay. We're going to get him!" But first these two dudes wound up selling us some good weed. They led us to an ATM and this time Lucas withdrew the cash. It was good shit, the kind we needed. It was a good time, you know what I mean? So we were in Miami for seven days. It was an epic trip. Lots of sex, lots of booze, and lots of smoke. All too soon it was time to go. Then we headed back to college for spring trimester.

We were back in party land! It was pretty much Sunday to Sunday going out. When we got back, I hooked up with this new girl named Kate, a girl I had always had a crush on. She wasn't really new because she was a friend of Brandon's. She was really cute and I wanted her in the worst way, so I told Brandon I needed to hit it off, you know what I mean? Hook me up! This was before Brandon got ejected from college. She lived three doors down from me in the dorms. It took Brandon forever to hook me up, and when I got back from Miami, it was smooth between me and Kate.

It was funny how we met. I had this poster in my dorm room. It said, "101 Sex Positions…Sex Every Day and Every Way". And when I was screwing a girl, I had them sign the position that we did. So this girl, Kate, signed off on a few of those positions! But when I finally did fuck her, I didn't even want it. By then she was more of a friend, you know? Still to this day I can feel that attraction, and I will always have something deep down for my sweet Kate.

Chapter 7

Back in Provi

The first week I get back from Miami was the first time I ever did cocaine. I'm sitting at the club with a few of my bros. It's me, Cheese and Milhem, and we're shooting the shit with Hanesworth and Randy. Randy and Hanesworth are like, "Yeah, you really gotta try some coke. Don't tell any of the brothers, and don't tell anybody in the fraternity that we're doing this, you know. Just try it once and never do it again." So "Yeah," I said, "I'm down, I'm down. Whatever." We were going to try it just once, see what the high was like, take notes, you know? And of course that was it because we loved cocaine so much. The Devil just reached in and grabbed me, as you'll see...

The second week of college, I forgot to tell you, I met this girl named Teresa, who lived in room 606. She was this crazy suicidal chick, but I didn't know that right away. When I first met her, she looked like she was 25, and she had this long jet black hair, nice Ed Hardy outfits, a massive ass, and she was just beautiful. I was like, "Wow! Who is this girl? I want to do her!"

I finally get to hit that off, and man, it was good! She was some crazy bitch in bed, and she kept me howling! We liked being with each other and the sex was fantastic, so we're hanging out a lot. We're going shopping, doing all this great stuff, and I even wound up meeting her family. But she turned out to be crazy! This girl ruffied me one night. I don't know what hit me or what she gave me, but I'm down for the count. When I wake up, she's staring at me, just very creepy.

We had our ups and downs, and we went through a lot of stuff, and it was like crazy. You don't really know what it's like to be with somebody who's nuts... Like with Teresa, she was beautiful and at times acted normal, but something was really wrong with her and it was only by hanging out with her that you could tell. A lot of people started hating me, like most of my sorority sisters. "You're taking advantage of Teresa?" they'd say. But it wasn't like that. It took me a while to realize that I had hooked up with a woman who was really fucked up. It's really not as simple as it seems and sometimes crazy people can act normal enough so you think their crazy is normal...and the crazy behavior comes on so slowly that you can't tell it's crazy until you start to see how crazy it's become. That's what happened to me.

If you didn't know Teresa, it was hard to tell how crazy she was. Teresa was just nuts, and she was very suicidal. She would have these blackout panic moments where she wouldn't remember anyone in the world. You could be her mom, and she wouldn't recognize you.

They say the crazy ones make the best sex, and she was definitely the greatest sex. And she was a great girl, but she was crazy. She took care of me, gave me whatever I needed or wanted, and she always did shit for me. Like I'd come back to my room and she'd have it cleaned. I could bring up other girls around her and she'd be mad, but she wouldn't say anything, you know what I mean? It was just that kind of scene.

By now I've had sex with 25 girls. In my first trimester, which is 11 weeks, I'd had sex with 12. That's one girl every week, average. So I'm doing my thing, man, meeting a bunch of girls. When I was pledging, I couldn't increase the number of sexual partners very quickly because I couldn't talk to anyone! We couldn't talk to any girls, guys, or anyone you were friends with, except your pledge brothers. So that put a damper on my numbers. But now, you see, that restriction was gone!

At this point it's getting close to St. Patty's Day, and we wound up having a toga social. The toga social was to help us get ready for St. Patty's Day. My fraternity brothers and sorority sisters were wearing next to nothing, you know, and everybody is into partying heavily and having a blast. I got my nipples pierced, and a few months later I even got my dick pierced. It was just like all-out party, all out ready for war, nonstop, we're just going and going. It happens that Teresa was my sorority sister as well. She had just got in the Sigma Delta Tau sorority, otherwise known as the "Suck Don't Talk" sorority. So she's like my pledge sister on top of being my fuck buddy.

And all my brothers at the toga social were like, "Oh! We can't fuck Vic's bitch," and my buddy Milhem was dating Teresa's pledge sister, who was Olivia. "Hey, everyone! We can't fuck Teresa or Olivia." Me and Joe were best friends 'cause we had sex with a lot of women. We were like two roosters set loose in a henhouse. We became very close early in the year when we were pledging and he told me he had fucked 18 girls and I had fucked 12, and it was only the third week of college. Milhem and I were like Starsky and Hutch; where there was one, there was the other. Our pledge brothers hated our scoring so much that they called us boyfriend and girlfriend! We fucked a lot of girls together at a lot of orgies. In his freshman year, Joe was called 'Interstate 95' because he had fucked 95 girls in one year of college, but it was his last year because he flunked out!

St. Patty's Day was our first bar crawl. There were 50 bars on our fraternity's list, and we had to have a shot and a beer at each bar.

The pub-crawl starts at 7:00 a.m. when all the guys meet up with matching t-shirts, and the pre-gaming starts with a bunch of eggs, kegs and alcohol. Everybody's putting some breakfast food in their bellies, everyone's got a handle, you know, there's cans of beer everywhere, and the girls are on their way. The bar crawl officially begins at 9:00 a.m. and lasts for 24 hours. Everybody winds up splitting off somewhere down the line. Some people make it, some people don't make it. Some people get arrested. Some people go to the hospital. Some people get into fights. You lose a lot of people. We started off with about 125, but only a few survived. I wound up making it to all the bars in my freshman year. It was a great ordeal, just to live through that crawl! I had about 19 shots and 32 beers...and I was on drugs, too. The next day you wake up at eight in the morning and you skip class, you know? We used to save up all our class absences for St. Patty's Day so we could go all out.

In my freshman and sophomore years the college allowed you two absences for each class before you got dropped. After that the administration got wise and changed it to no absences. In my freshman year we saved up our absences for afterschool specials, which is like when you get a keg, and the sorority girls come to the fraternity. Everybody gets hammered all day long, and then we fuck the girls all night. And fuck them again. You know what I mean?

Okay, so now alumni weekend is coming up. All the fraternity brothers have jobs to do. The first two positions I held was alumni chair, and rush chair. My task as rush chair was going out and inviting pledges for next year; as the alumni chair I had to keep in touch with a few hundred alumni, get the alumni weekend set up, make sure the parties in the clubs were organized and that everything is being done right, like making flyers and all that kind of shit.

So that's how the freshman year ended. Alumni weekend worked out...I did more work for this event than all the coursework I did all year long for my classes! I got an A in alumni weekend! College was surreal to me...I didn't know what the fuck was going on in the classes, and it's amazing to me that I didn't flunk out. I did no work but I came out with a 3.0. I don't know how I did that. I swear, I never studied, I never did anything. I never bought books in college after my first trimester. And I never purchased a textbook ever again. But JWU was a Top Ten party college, so I guess I was meeting and exceeding college standards. With all the drugs, alcohol and sex I was enjoying, I might make valedicktorian yet!

A couple of things to mention…My pledge master was Matty Mills, and he was just a big juice head, a fucking redheaded ape from Yonkers, New York who was insanely crazy. Matt got stabbed once in ten places and kept fighting, throwing down his attackers! This motherfucker was fucking insane, a big jacked-up McGyver. He was muscular, and turbocharged like a rhino. Nothing could stop him when he got cranked up. He was amazing to watch. But he wound up bailing on us after he graduated, which was that year. It was tough to lose him…he just vaporized. He did all this reckless shit to us, and it was all for nothing. We don't have a close bond with him anymore, or even know where the fuck he is.

Another brother was Zohan; he was from Hungary, and he was the assistant pledge master under Mills. Zohan was the man, and I always went out with him. We had a ton of adventures, and we did a lot of drugs together. He was a great dude, and is still one of my greatest friends.

Chapter 8

Summertime, and the Living is Sleazy

After the alumni weekend, it was pretty much the end of the school year and it was time to move out of the dorms. It was one of the hardest things, you know? You're living with these kids all year, having a wild time every day, and all of a sudden it's like, damn, man, what the fuck? But screw it, we were all about to get apartments now. So I'm on my way out the door, moving into my fraternity house. Of my group, it's only going to be me. Cheese bailed, Milhem bailed, and Trotta bailed. Nobody wanted to live at the house, so instead I'm living with Sabby, Luke, Tony Danza and Randy.

It was summertime! My first summer on my own, living in Providence. If you know East Coast summers, you know it's hot and humid, and the air is so thick it's like you're swimming. Then you get these sudden summer storms, with thunder and lightning, and the air is lighter for a little while until the tension builds up again. And it was hot…during the day the pavement radiates heat under your sandals, and at night you're praying for a soft breeze to cool you down.

I got all my shit moved into the house…it was a place to be even if it was rundown and had rodents. Hell, it was part of the adventure! I had a lot of brothers around me, lots of weed, cocaine on the sly, and plenty of SDT sisters to roll around with. Heaven in spite of the heat.

We had these Puerto Rican neighbors who were always fucked up and they're like these wild savages. They are sort of living off us, taking our beer and food and shit like that, but whatever. So we're living in the fraternity house and I met one of my alumni named Myles. It turns out that me and Myles are from the same hometown but I had never seen him before.

Myles tells me, "Hey, Vic, let's make some cash this summer!" I give him my usual response, which is "Whatever! I'm down." So I wind up getting about 4,000 pills from Myles. I mean I had every fucking drug you can name, from Percocet to Xanax to muscle relaxers to Vicodin! I had everything you could imagine. So it's going to be one hell of a busy summer, and I'm all about making some serious money, you know, to help out Myles. I'm also doing these drugs as well as selling them.

I found myself starting to get into the pill game, and it was like, holy shit, I was blowing five, six, seven bennies in the morning, and then going to the gym to work out. I was on fucking steroids, man. It was making me crazy, and I don't know how the fuck my body made it through this shit. I'm on fucking 'roids, and I went from being 125 pounds to 162.5 pounds. I found myself going a little nuts in the head. It was too many drugs. And it wasn't just the shit I had going on in my brain and body, either. Shit! I had people knocking on my window in the fraternity house trying to get hold of me. Junkies coming to get this and junkies coming to get that! Fucking junkies, man! I couldn't get any rest. There was always some asshole looking for me so they could get high. I was making cash, sure, but I was hunted!

I wound up getting arrested. I was drinking every morning at the Alpha Sigma Tau house with Chloe, Carla Dee, and Fellon Ellen aka Hitler. These were hot honeys and we were having margarita mornings and getting hammered. These sisters were the biggest drinkers on campus. It was like, shit, nonstop. I went from one fire to the next and I was getting fucking toasted!

So one of my brothers, Biancony aka Dirty Cony, is fucked up on Percocet 30s blues, which are called Little Blue Guys, or' Those Fucking Things'. Biancony was a trippy dude. His favorite line was, "Yeah, you dirty bitches! Like prove it, you dirty whores!"

And, you know, we're riding around, and we have a bunch of pills on us. A cop pulls us over for loud music, which wasn't too smart, but we were high. I wound up giving the cops my fake ID and they ran the information. Everything was good, and as we're about to get let off, one cop says, "I know this little fucker from somewhere... Let me see your tattoos." He looked at my tattoos and that was it. They took me right there.

As it happens, my parents are in Providence that weekend to visit. I didn't want my parents to hear about my getting arrested, so I wound up running from the cops. The cops had horses, and I'm hammered, but I'm so drunk I'm running from them. I had flip-flops on and baggy shorts so it was hard to run, but I wound up getting away. Then I'm like, you know what? I better stop because my buddy, you know, Biancony, I don't know what he's going to say, and I didn't want to get into more trouble. So I turned back around and they wound up taking me to jail for the night. I woke up in the morning, I have no flip-flops because they disappeared, and I'm walking into the courthouse looking scruffy as shit, hung over, shoeless, and whatever. And my parents aren't getting me out of there. They were totally freaked out and disgusted with me. Well, so was I, and I was a mess. I never went back into that courthouse ever again.

That summer was reckless. There was a lot of shit going on. Like the one time me and Sabby both lost our phones during a seven-day binge... seven days getting fucked up like, I mean, literally, going to bed at 8:00 a.m. and waking up an hour later to keep on drinking. Man, that was a summer to remember...and I wish I could!

We were up 13 hours, talking shit. We were all on pills and drugs, and I was like the Goodie Bag man, so you would come to me and I would have a variety of drugs I was going to serve you. I didn't need to sell drugs; that was the funny thing about it. I really wasn't doing it for the money, though that's what Myles wanted. I was doing this more because it was going on, it was happening, it was the scene I was in, and as usual...I was down.

But then my grandmother died.

I loved my grandmother. She was loving and kind, and she was like an angel on Earth. I couldn't believe she was gone, you know?

I remember getting very, very fucked up. I stayed up all night with my friends and a couple of girls, and we literally blew seven or eight 8-balls of coke in a few hours. Now I'm completely fucked up, and I have to catch a train from Providence to Jersey. I'm edgy, totally wired on this train, coked out of my mind, and I get to Jersey for the funeral.

I find myself blowing Vicodin in the bathroom at the place where the family gathered. I was really fucked up. My grandmother had just died, I don't really want to be here, I want to be back in the fraternity house with my friends and shit having a good time. Instead I'm with this somber bunch of people; we're talking about Grandma, visiting the casket, making small talk, playing roles. It was awful.

Of course I wound up getting into it with my family. I'm not really that close to my cousins and all that kind of stuff. I don't really like them, and growing up they just weren't my kind of people. They don't have much going for themselves in their life and one thing led to another and I got into a fight with these guys. I remember I left; it was like 3:00 in the morning. I went to the home of one of my friends from college and I stayed there overnight. The funeral was at 8:00 a.m. I went to the service and then I left. Ashley, one of my sorority sisters, picked me up. We went over to my buddy Loeb's house; he was a real good friend of mine. We smoked a blunt and then Ashley drove me back to Prov. I was just so pissed off. And I was hammered. I wasn't in my right mind from all the drugs, booze, and the emotional crisis I was in.

I got back to Providence, and everyone was partying and ready to go out just like always, and I wound up passing out on the front steps of the fraternity. You would have thought I was dead. It was like my body had no more energy to run, you know. I was blowing Zanny's, I was blowing Vicodin, I was blowing cocaine, I had uppers and downers, and my body just shut down. I wound up going to sleep. My brothers had to carry me into my room. I was unconscious.

Eventually I came around and started up again. I find out that my cousin Chuck was here, and he was going to live at the house with me for the summer since he was returning to college after taking a break. So he's in the house, and my fraternity brother Danza and all his reckless friends Jelly Bean, Nick and Danny are there and they got fucked up. They trashed the house. It was unbelievable! And they tried to kill my cousin. They were hostile and arrogant, like "Move your car, you nigger!" and they were just going off and didn't even know what they were doing.

The next morning I flipped out on my dude, Danza, and I'm like, "Dude, what the fuck are you doing, bro? You've got the kitchen table and everything out in the street! What the fuck!"

I mean they threw the entire kitchen table, beds, everything in the house out into the middle of the street! They went off like a bomb! I don't know what drugs or other shit they were doing, but the whole entire living room, kitchen and other parts of the house were in the middle of the fucking street, right there in the middle of downtown Providence! It was just crazy, trying to live through all this insanity.

By the end of the summer my cousin finally got his own apartment, and everything began to shift again. It was time for the new school year.

Sophomore Year

Chapter 9

My Favorite Year of College!

The summer ended with my grandmother's dying. It was such a hard time, man. I loved her so much. There were all those memories…the sweet times, all the stuff you remember as a kid with the food, the laughter, and most of all, the love. Those feelings, man. When someone close to you dies, it's like a part of you dies with them, the part that connected you. I know you carry that person in your heart. I get that. But it's just not the same. It's all different. And everyone handles their pain in the way they can, the way they have to. I went to my grandmother's funeral coked out.

My crew had just got moved into our new apartments and everything, getting ready for the new school year, and I was at the Washington Street house. That was the day I had planned to move my furniture in, but that was also when my mom called and told me my grandma had died; I would be joining my family the next day and then going to the funeral. So me and my crew stayed up all that night with a bunch of girls and we blew, oh, had to be about three 8-balls of cocaine, you know what I mean? I was feeling down in the dumps, man, really low. Drugging was my answer.

Once I got back from the funeral, I flushed all the drugs down the toilet, and I gave a bunch of them away. I was just kind of dumping the drug scene. I could see how drugs and shit were affecting me, and I knew my grandma wouldn't approve, so I figured it was my sophomore year and time to start a new slate.

I moved out of my fraternity house that September, even though I had just moved in. I couldn't stay there anymore, and was only there for the summer.

The first month of school was terrible. I couldn't sleep, I couldn't do anything, I needed my personal space, you know? I had girls coming into my room all the time, and I've got brothers kicking the door down while I'm in there having sex! It was crazy.

So I moved out of there and moved in with one of my alumni brothers, that dude named Myles. He was the guy I was selling drugs with during the summer, and I moved into my new apartment with him. It was cool, it was like damn, I had my own space and privacy, and I didn't have to worry about being in mid-stroke with a camera suddenly filming my butt, you know?

I liked living with Myles; we were going to be laid back and smoke weed all the time and whatever, but when I got there, you know, I started to notice I was like going downhill again. I had just given away and flushed away all the fucking drugs I'd been selling with Myles, but I'd wake up in the morning and have Kilotopin and weed waiting for me! I couldn't easily control my desires, and I would just get fucked up, you know what I'm saying? The shit was just too handy, too available. And I wanted it...I liked being high even though I didn't want to get high. So it was bad, it was bad, you know?

When I saw what was happening to me, I knew I needed to get out of Dodge. My cousin also started to notice what was going on, and he encouraged me to get loose. At that time me and Beth were together and just getting serious.

So my pledge brothers, Chowder and Nick, were living in this apartment complex, and Beth lived there, too. Chowder and Nick were like, yo, there's a three-bedroom apartment upstairs, let's go ahead and grab that. I said, oh, that's awesome. We check everything out, and I wind up moving into that apartment with them, with Beth in her own place downstairs. Now I've moved three times in the span of three months. You know what I mean? I'm like damn, I'm just moving around! If you've ever moved your shit a lot, you know what a pain in the ass it is. Few things are as bad as moving, with the boxes, packing, unpacking, losing shit, everything getting all fucked up...

But anyway, I get over to the new apartment and I felt a lot more comfortable. I spoke to Myles and he was a little mad about me moving out of his place, but you know, I had to do what I had to do. I was getting screwed up with drugs. Even so, I wound up growing a pot plant in my new place. I started it from a seed...had a grow light on it, watered it faithfully...and it began to grow, eventually up to five feet high. It was fun nipping bud off it from time to time. Pretty good high, too.

In the midst of all this going on, the Washington Street crew was just getting heavy. We had our whole team, and we were going out every weekend, having a great time, partying our asses off …and that's when things started falling apart. You couldn't tell it right away, but that was the start. One day, three felons were living on our couch.

These three dudes were Milla's cousins. Milla brought them up and at the time, we didn't know they were felons. The leader's name was A. That was his name…A. Just A. I never knew him by any other name. I later found out he had done a seven-year stretch in prison and had just got out of there when he parked his ass on our couch. He was a scary looking dude, you know? He was only an inch taller than me, but he had a big head and a thick neck, and his eyes were glassy. His pupils sort of hung at the top of his eyeballs. When he looked at you, you kind of froze like you were staring at a king cobra. One scary son of a bitch.

His two henchmen were Dappa and Fat Boy. Dappa was another scary asshole. He was like 14 years old, tall and skinny, but you didn't want to mess with him, either. Usually the young skinny kids are more dangerous than the adults. Fat Boy was the other enforcer, and he was as nasty looking as A. Yeah, he was fat. If you saw these three coming at you, you'd want to give them a wide berth.

The other guy who was part of their crew was Money Mike. He was a rich white kid who was their driver. Money Mike drove these three felons wherever they needed to go. I never learned how or why Money Mike hung out with these dudes, but wherever they were, he usually was, too…except for one time, which I'll explain later. Money Mike was a handsome dude, though. He had a big square jaw, high forehead, nice smile; the kind of guy you'd expect to find crewing on a World Cup sailing ship.

So one day we had these three felons that we just don't even know living on our couch at the Washington Street house, courtesy of Milla. That was fucking weird. And they brought up packages and garbage bags full of drugs; they brought up everything, and we all sat down and had a huge meeting, and we, like, built an empire. Nothing was moving, no drug in Providence was moving unless it was coming from one of our guys.

It turns out that we were working for some well-positioned people who were connected to heavy players. We were the college-scene distribution network in Providence. In Rhode Island, my buddy, Nick, well, his dad is very well tied. I've known the Italian mobsters, a couple of those guys, since my freshman year. We were living on their turf, on Federal Hill, which is an all-Italian area. So we were protected. The only thing that did happen was we started noticing a lot of activity, a lot of feds, you know what I'm saying? So that's when it started getting rowdy, it started getting tied up.

But anyway, we were allowed to operate without any problems, and besides, I wasn't out there like that. I had other people working for me. There was no way that I was going to put my face out there, and my hands were clean. All the drugs were coming through Milla's cousins, and the mob was getting their cut. A ran Massachusetts, and now he was running Providence.

Pittsfield, Massachusetts is a small town in Berkshire County; it's where Milla was from. There are a lot of druggies up there so A had a lot of product coming in. We had product coming in from Georgia, from Massachusetts, and from Brooklyn. So A, Dappa and Fat Boy brought up all of their stuff, and P-Money was also bringing in drugs from his own sources. We were taking trips back home to get more and more stuff. Then we started meeting older people back home who had their stuff, which was the prescribed shit we needed. So now we had the street drugs and we also had the prescription drugs.

Prescription drugs were very, very big when I was in college, especially during my freshman and sophomore years. Percocet 30s, which we called Blues, and "Those Little Thin Things", or "Those Little Guys", those were very popular. A lot of kids wound up in the emergency room, and some even died from them. Some kids just did too many, and never woke up.

The drugs were arriving at our Washington Street house in mass quantities. This was thanks to A who pretty much started it off with his deep connections.

Also, the rave scene was just starting to come on, the big rave parties with the flashing neon lights, pumped-up music and wild dancing, and flowing with alcohol and drugs, and this was my scene, man, and I was able to mingle with all the girls and sell them tons of ecstasy. Like, I mean, I was selling 400 – 500 ecstasy pills every two days, every two to three days. One day I did a pack of 600 in 20 minutes. And then we had to drive all the way back to New York to resupply because there was a big rave called Day-Glo and people were getting 50-packs off me, so I moved 600 of them in 20 minutes. I had to take a trip back to Connecticut down to that kid Money Mike's house; A took us to MM's house. There were more pills there, there were another like, 1200 of them, and we brought them up. We didn't move all of those that day but, you know, we moved a lot of them.

As far as cocaine went, we had ounces of cocaine, ounces and ounces. I'm not going to say we had pounds or kilos, but everything added up and we had all of that, too. We pretty much had kilos of coke, we had massive amounts of marijuana. So pretty much with the marijuana, that's when Kiss comes into the story. We called this kid Kiss because he loved the stuff like Jadakiss, and he was bringing up pounds and pounds of weed from his connection, and his connection was in the Triads, the Asian mob in Springfield, Massachusetts. So we were definitely well-connected, we were good, you know?

Like I said, things slowly started falling apart... We all went out to the bar one night, it was all 45 of us, it was 15 girls and 30 dudes. And we were all getting ready to go to Club Ultra...we were all pre-gaming and everything. And, you know, it seemed like a great night but you just knew something bad was going to happen. You could just tell, you know? So pretty much we go out and then some crazy shit started happening.

Alizabeth got a tooth knocked out by a bouncer, I pass out drunk, you know, whatever. A fight starts and it turns into a big riot. That kind of shit...which is almost normal for us. But then Kiss gets into a fight with his girlfriend, and he's speeding out of our driveway, and he blows a bunch of snow into the cop's face as he speeds off, and he didn't even know it was a cop behind him. The police cruiser had to slam on its brakes as Kiss's green Nissan suddenly backed onto the street and slid out onto the road. Kiss sped through a stop sign, but was brought to a stop at the PC Mart. The sergeant frisked Kiss and found a bag of weed in his pockets, then searched the car and discovered about 10 pounds more, along with about $5,000 in cash! Kiss was charged with possession of the kilos, plus failing to stop at the stop sign, and, oh, yeah, not using his turn signal!

Since Kiss had come tearing out of the Eaton Street house, now the cops know our house, they know this one house, you know? Kiss, he's our boy; we know he's a softy, you know what I mean? But the thing is his dad is mob connected, so Kiss beats that whole case. He was looking at two to five years of jail time. They found the 10 pounds of weed, they found a bunch of pills, they found a lot of stuff on him, but he beat all that. He got off with just probation. Even so, Kiss wound up getting in trouble again and again, and that started leading stuff back to us. So now A, instead of staying at the Washington Street house, which was a drug house, this felon and his crew moved into my apartment to avoid the heat that was coming down on the Washington Street house!

My apartment was this spot where, like, we could keep shit outside of the drug house, you know what I mean? We knew we were good at my house. I had just a basic apartment, never too many people, just a lot of girls coming over, hanging out, but never really had people coming in and out of my house for drugs, nothing, so it was a cool place and kept the heat away from me. But I was really unhappy when A and his crew moved into my place. And you can't say no to A.

At this point we were selling massive amounts of drugs. I wound up helping one of my buddies from home. He needed some help with his college application, so I did his paperwork and he wound up moving to Providence; his name was Wi-Fi and now he was part of my crew.

Muggs and Rainstorm, they started dating during my sophomore year. And when they blew up, that pretty much broke apart the entire crew, you know? We had 15 girls, Rainstorm's girls, and we had our boys, and we all hung out having a blast, and these two started dating… but as soon as they started arguing, then no one wanted to hang out anymore, the girls began arguing with each other, and everything just kind of turned to shit and the group split up.

Chapter 10

Heading Downhill Fast

So now I'm seeing everything go downhill. You got the junkies like Bobo and Adam and these guys, you know, they're just junking out. And Muggs and Rainstorm fell apart. And the heat is getting turned up.

And now me and Trups wind up getting into a fight, and here's why. A lot of stuff started going missing out of the house. You know, Milla brought up his boy, a kid named Tweener. Milla brings him up from the town and all of Muggs's stuff starts going missing. Muggs always had everything, he always had good stuff, you know? And he was the kind of kid who would do anything for you, but the second he got mad, Muggs would throw it all back in your face. You had to be careful what you asked him for because later that shit would come back at you like, "You mugs be trying to use and abuse me!" which is how he got his name, or my favorite one, "Good one, dude, what is this? A charity?"

So all of Muggs's stuff starts going missing, shit like jeans, his iPad, earrings...like real diamond earrings, computers, and even his fucking Lexus got stolen. His Lexus got stolen in the middle of the night. He thought it was all of us in the house, he thought somebody set him up and had his car taken. We wound up finding it in our senior year, but that's later in the story. So this was a mass event going on. Muggs's shit was disappearing. Was it the two junkies? We didn't know. And then my shit began disappearing, too. Fuck!

Me and Trups, he was my boy, like, I was hanging out with him every day, you know what I'm saying? I would always hang out with Trups; we lived across the street from each other. We were tight, and he was like my brother, always staying at my apartment, and we had pretty much the same classes.

One day I wound up getting into his car; he left me his whip because he was going home for the week. I get in and holy shit! All my stuff, a whole shitload of stuff I'd been looking for that had gone missing from my apartment is in his car! It was stolen. And Trups had stolen it! So I'm like, wow, man! This kid really stole from me and I'm hanging out with them every day, you know?

That night I went to a little party. I had Trups's car, you know, and I was whipping around, and I pulled up to the party. The whole crew of us were there, and we roll up with a brand-new Maxima tinted the hell out, and we've got a Lexus, and an Infinity, a Honda, and one of us had a Jeep. So every time we roll up, we're coming in, all 30 of us, coming in deep, you know what I mean? The junkies' job was to go in and find other junkies and sell stuff; our job was to sit back, look cool, visualize what's going on and get the girls.

That night I got to the party and I told P-Money, I said, "Yo, P-Money, I'm going to fuck Trups's girl." And he was like, "No, Vic, you're not. No you're not, bro."

He didn't know I wanted to do this out of revenge. I mean, this fucking bastard is stealing my shit, and Muggs's shit, and we're hanging out like brothers? He's doing shit to me? Fuck him, man. I was going to do some shit to him.

So I go up to Linda, and I'm like, "Hey, Linda, when are we fucking?" You know?

And she's like, "Shut up, Vic. Where is Muggs?"

And I'm like, "Yo, like, you know, he's clearly back home right now."

She says, "Well, Vic...you know, to be honest with you, I've always wanted to fuck you and P-Money."

You know what I mean? Out of all of his friends, Linda has the hots for me and P-Money! She had reddish hair, a big smile, and was super playful...plus she had a nice rack, you know what I mean? Okay, cool. Let's get started!

So I brought her into the corner. Me and P-Money both start hooking up with this chick, whatever. I wind up going upstairs with her. Linda wanted to have a threesome, but P-Money said no, he wasn't down for that, so I'm like whatever. I go upstairs with Linda because I wanted to have sex with her. And I did; she was great in bed and I had my revenge.

Now, word doesn't get out to Trups for awhile, but what happened was that kid Kiss, the kid who got arrested for having 10 pounds of weed in his car, well, he got kicked out of school for that arrest, and in the midst of all of that shit, Milla told Kiss what happened. So, Kiss blabs and tells everybody, "Yo, guys, Vic smashed Trups's girl!" and whatever. So Kiss is back home, and Turbs hits on Linda's best friend, which Is Marie. Marie is Kiss's girlfriend from back home, and they came to college dating together, and Turbs wound up hitting it with Marie.

I don't remember how, but this turned into a big feud, like Vic and Turbs are fucking over everybody, their fucking everybody's girls, so when Kiss found out that Turbs smashed Marie, he got really mad about it. He told Trups that I fucked Linda. So now Trups wasn't talking to me anymore, you know. But, the way that they found out, was Milla was coming back with a big package from his town. So we were waiting for this big package that morning; we had about five or six kilos coming in. Things had been dry, and now we were about to get back up on our feet. So Milla's coming in with this package, and we're telling him no, don't come, it's hot. The cops are here. But we were telling him not to come because we knew Marie was in the house with Turbs. So Milla said, "Guys, Kiss's boys want me to drop their stuff off. Let them in the house Guy." We let Kiss's boys in the house, and Marie was coming down the stairs in her underwear so they put two and two together, and they hit up Kiss and told him, "Yo, we saw your chick there."

Of course, Kiss was freaking mad about it. So he sent a bunch of kids to come down and fuck up Turbs's car. They poured bleach all over his car, smashed out every window, and this was in the middle of winter, so this kid had no windows, no nothing. You know, Turbs was a pretty broke kid, you know what I mean? Like very broke. So broke that he never got the window fixed until like later on that year.

Then me, Cheese, and Milla, we go to this big frickin' party at this place the fraternity rented out in Massachusetts. We take a bunch of party buses up there, to this place called The Mint Lounge. Whatever. I wound up getting completely hammered, of course. On the way back, I remember waking up when we get to the gas station near the Washington Street house; we're about to go to an after-hour party.

I remember Trups was outside our car. When I got out of the car, he was like, "Dude!" He was moving like he wanted to fight. I knew he knew I'd balled his girl, so I figured he had it in for me. So I pretty much started boxing with him. I hit him with a three piece. You know what I mean? One, two, a combo to the face, we were just playing around, and then I just got back into the car, and I went back to sleep. I was hammered. But his blood was up and he was just flipping out. "Fuck you, Vic! I'll fight you, Vic, right now!"

Me and Trups wound up getting into a fight, and it wound up being like a draw, kind of; it wasn't really a fight. You know what I mean? And that's when the whole scene changed and everybody split up, and we all went our separate ways because siding with Trups was Adam the junky, and Adam pulled all the junkies over to his side, and then there was me, and a few kids took my side, you know, but everybody started splitting up, one by one, little by little. Still, it was Trups who had been the thief first, and I was just stealing back my own.

After the fight, me and Trups eventually wound up being cool again with each other; you know a month after, two months after. We had been too tight to throw away the connection we had, not over a fricking girl, you know? It's like dudes understand this shit. Yes, we're possessive over the girls we like who do us, but there are too many girls who will, so why screw up a good relationship with a brother? You know? If Linda was like that, and she was, then I actually did us both a favor. And I got all my shit back, too.

Meanwhile, our local felon is still in the picture; A is bringing up more and more and more. I told A that my family had a house in the Poconos, and he said, "Yeah? Yo! My cousin lives in the Poconos." I said, "No, he doesn't, man!" A insisted, "Yeah, he does!" All right, so I wind up meeting A in the Poconos! Like this is a drug selling goon who's living with me in Providence, and now I'm like, "Dude, you're going to be with me in the Poconos?"

I knew this kid from my hometown, and I had told him what I was doing, you know, so now he and some of my old buddies from my hometown wanted to come up to Prov for New Year's…see what it was like in town, so here they come…and that felt weird. I stopped at A's house in the morning before we left the Poconos for Providence and A drops about 5 ounces of coke on me. Shit! I had to split it with Milla when I got back to Providence. And I literally had 2,000 e-pills or so. So we're driving all this stuff back to Prov for four hours, whatever.

I'm bringing my hometown buddies back. And now this is starting to feel really weird. I kind of started to see that I didn't really like my old friends from home anymore. I guess they're forced upon you, you know? It's like family, like those people are also forced upon you, too. You grow up with them and all that kind of stuff, but at some point you see you don't connect with them anymore. Your friends from college, that's different…you meet these kids and they're the same as you, doing the same shit as you, but my friends from home aren't the same as me anymore. We've all changed, or they've stayed the same and I haven't. We always said we were the same because we grew up together, lived in the same area, went to the same school and that kind of shit, but as you get older, as life leads you along, you realize they're not the same as you after all. So I'm bringing these kids up, and I really didn't want them there, you know what I mean? You could see the change in me, like fuck these kids. Kind of like that. Fucked up, but fuck it. I never went out of my way to see them, ever again. I was done with them.

So now it's Valentine's Day. This is big, this is funny. So Cheese says, "Yo, I'm talking to this girl named Jade Kindle. She's hot!" And I'm like, "Dude, get the fuck out of here. I tried to hit her up, you know, at the beginning of last year, when I was a freshman moving into the dorms. She didn't even hit me back up, you know?"

He denied me: "I'm telling you, I'm talking to her, we have a date and everything." So I'm like, "Dude, let me see this bitch. You've got to bring her around."

So for about a week this is going on and now it's Valentine's Day. We go shopping for our girls, and I'm shopping for Beth. Cheese winds up getting this Jade Kindle bitch a bunch of stuff.

So my boy, the kid I brought up from home, Wi-Fi, he was like, "Vic, this girl went to our rival high school back home." I'm like, "Bro, shut up!" "No, I swear to God!" So we check the name Jade Kindle on Facebook and about 1,500 of them popped up. Now we're like, oh, okay. So Cheese is getting played. He's being catfished, you know? This chick wasn't real…but who the fuck was it?

Cheese keeps telling us he's been at this chick's house, he met her mom, he's been hanging out with her, and everything. Come to find out, this chick is totally fake. I called one of my buddies from back home and he told me. This dude says Cheese is talking to some dude from my rival high school, this gay kid! And he's here in Prov, at JWU's culinary program, probably sticking his biscuits in someone's oven, if you know what I mean.

I like see this kid in one of the JWU dining halls, you know, he's one of the chefs, and he's like, "Yeah, yeah, I hang out with one of your pals, Cheese, all the time. We're like hanging out tonight. I'll be toking with him tonight." And later Cheese told me and the guys , "Yo, I can't hang out tonight, bro. I'm going to Jade Kindle's. I'm going to her house." That's what made us think that Cheese was a fag.

I had a class with Cheese at the time, and we got to class and he was pretty much like, "You know, like are you calling me gay and shit?" And I said, "Dude, are you a homo? Like, you know what I mean, why don't you just tell us?" And he's like, "You know what? There are a lot of things you don't know about me." He didn't say no. He never did. Sometimes you have to let a gay guy figure it out on his own; and if he wants to stay in the closet even though everyone can see what he won't say, you let him be.

There's more to this story in the senior year. To this day we all still think something is up with him. Anyway, Cheese wasn't talking to me for a while. I don't know what happened but he got over it, and after a while he came into the house one day and said, "You guys want to go to Hawaii?"

Chapter 11

The Trip from Hell

So of course we're down. It's spring break and we want to be where it's warm; last year it was Miami and I was swap-fucking Beth and Amber with my boy Lucas; this year it would be Hawaii. Who knew what lay in store for us? It was going to be kickass!

We had a bunch of drugs to sell, and we were on the money. We're still moving massive amounts of drugs. You know, we were running it. Everything was smooth, pretty much, so yeah, we're down to go to Hawaii.

Cheese tells us it's like $600 round-trip, and the hotel is included. Turbs and P-Money said they wouldn't go, they said that was stupid, there was something not up with it, you know, something not right. And that was true...but I didn't think twice about it, so me, Cheese, and Milla are good to go. Awesome!

It's time to leave for Hawaii, and Milla is supposed to be ready. Me and Cheese are ready to go. Cheese is staying in my apartment, and we get a nice little limo to get us to the airport. Out at the Washington Street residence, the kids that are living there are P-Money, Muggs, Milla, and Turbs. Those were the people that lived in that house, but it was everybody's house. That's where everyone was always at. So we went to pick up Milla and Milla was having this huge party with a bunch of his boys at the Washington Street house. He's leaving them there that morning while we go on vacation knowing that a lot of stuff has been getting stolen. We have over $10,000-$15,000 worth of product sitting there in the house, and you're going to leave these kids here, you know what I mean? Okay, bro...it's on you.

We get Milla and we finally break free of the party and head to the airport, catching our flight to Minnesota. We get to Minnesota and now we're stuck in the airport due to weather. Okay, okay. Not too bad. After a delay, we leave Minnesota and then arrive in Arizona. In Arizona, we watch as our plane takes off. We don't know that until we get to the check-in counter, and the attendants are pretty much like, well, dude, since there were weather conditions in Minnesota, you freaking missed your flight out, right? Now you're kind of like screwed until tomorrow. You have to buy a hotel and settle in for the night. We're like, no, we got stuck in Minnesota, and we were told it was a mechanical issue with the plane, so that puts it back on you, bitch. They said all right, cool. They gave us hotel vouchers and meal vouchers. The pussies.

Since we're in Arizona we call up Rainstorm, Muggs's girl, and we hit up Nicole and a couple of other girls we know who live there. They pick us up at the airport and we meet up with my aunt at our hotel, who also lives in Arizona. Aunt Lydia takes us out to eat and stuff, and then we go shopping. All our clothes are on the plane that's heading for Hawaii, and all we have is cash and a our carry-ons, so we go shopping. It turns out that Cheese is Jewish, so no disrespect, but he starts acting really stingy. I mean Cheese was really fucking cheap. There's not even a word for how cheap he was! We're getting clothes for the next two days and he asks me if we can go half on a pack of underwear. There's like two or three boxers in a pack for $10. I said, fucking no, dude. What if we get stuck here another day? You know what I mean? I need boxers, and he's like, well, bro, fuck you. He was all angry at me.

Yeah, I'm going full-blown shopping, I'm going to get pants for the night, me and Milla are going out to the clubs, you know, we found a couple of good spots to go to, and we got the girls to run with, so we get back to the hotel and we're getting dressed to go out. Cheese says, "I don't want to go out. I'm staying in."

"Well, dude, this is the first time you've been in Arizona, you know what I mean? We're stuck here and it's spring break. Let's just go out and spend a few bucks!" No, not Cheese. He's staying in with the TV remote. Jeez.

We get to this one crazy place, this really weird place on Scottsdale Avenue called American Junkie and Smash Box. Half of it's a club, the other half is a bar. Biggest bar in Scottsdale. So we get to this place, we're waiting in line and we see these girls from Milla's hometown back in Massachusetts. They live here now, going to college or some such shit. Milla kept saying he knew some girls out here and of all the crazy-ass things, here they are. They were here because it was this one girl's birthday.

So we now walk in, and we're just killing it, you know what I mean? We get into this bar, and I've never been in a bar where there are two dollar Petron shots. 80 proof tequila for two fucking dollars. We're taking these down all night. Then there is this big wheel, a spin-the-wheel kind of thing, and every five minutes there is a horn that goes off and a new girl is picked to get on the stage. The girl spins the wheel and whatever that wheel says, she has to do to me or I have to do to her. You know what I mean? Some of the things on the wheel were show your tits, kiss the guys in the front row, buy a stranger a drink, just little things like that, it wasn't serious stuff, but it was fun, you know?

The night gets on, and at some point me and Milla kiss the girls goodnight, leave there, and we happen to get into the cab of this crazy taxi driver from New York. This guy's pretty glad to see us because we're like home boys to this dude. He's in fucking Arizona, so he lights up with anyone who's from the East Coast. We're in his cab and we smell weed, so we ask him, bro, do you know where we can get some trees, just for the night?

He says, "You know what, since you guys are from home…" Me and Milla felt things were getting sketchy because the dude was taking us way out of the way, pretty much, from our hotel, and we were driving around, like on the edge of the desert, and we're hanging out smoking some shit. We don't even know this guy, and he's like, yeah, man, you guys are cool.

He pulls over his cab, opens up his trunk, we get out, and now we're in the middle of the fucking desert. It's pitch black out, the stars are like a stream of diamonds overhead, there's that chill from the desert, and nothing but silence… We look in this man's trunk, and he's got massive amounts of marijuana in there, like he had pounds and pounds and pounds, so he wound up just giving some to me and Milla.

He said, "Yeah, don't worry about the taxi ride. Give me 20 bucks and I'll give you guys a handful of weed from each stash I have here. It's all different kinds of shit, you know, like local and imported." So I said all right. So he gives us a mix of great shit, and we hung out with him, you know, and we smoked our asses off all night, just riding around somewhere in the desert outside Scottsdale.

The next morning, you know, we have to catch our flight. We get back to the hotel around dawn and I knock out. I lock my door with the chain. Milla had to break my hotel door in the morning so he could get me up so we could make it to the airport on time. We get to the airport and Milla had to go to the Western Union office to pick up some cash that was sent to him, and Cheese is like "Let's go get our tickets." We pick up our tickets at the counter, but Milla has no ticket. Milla's ticket is not there. "Ticket not found." So Cheese is "Yo, listen, let's just leave him and you know, tell him we boarded the plane already. You know? We'll call him in Hawaii." I'm like, "Bro, how are we going to leave this kid in Arizona?" You know what I mean? Cheese is like, "Bro, Katina and them, they can pick him up. I'll just give him the trip money back." I'm like, "Dude, we can't do that."

As we're talking this shit over, Milla is running down the stairs, like ready to go, and he's yelling, "Guys I got my money! Let's go! Where's my ticket?" And he sees my face and he's like, "Guys, what's going on, guy?"

That's Milla's favorite word, 'guy'. Guy, or kidder. Something weird, just weird things like that.

And I'm like, "Bro, like you don't have any ticket. These assholes fucked it up." So were trying to figure this out and Cheese is like "Fuck it, I'm out, I'm going to Hawaii. You guys can stay here." Milla says, "Okay, we'll all go to LA instead. Just give me my $600 back." And Cheese says, "No, I'll give you that when I get back from Hawaii." Milla says, "No you're not, bro."

So shit. We go to the counter; we tell the lady what's going on, and she said, "You guys have tickets so you can fly, but Milla only has a standby ticket. That means he could wait here for a week until there is a free seat. I doubt if you'll be able to get a plane out of here on standby because it is spring break. All the planes are pretty much full."

She gets her ass in gear and pulled some strings and there was someone who was supposed to leave 13 hours later. This agent trades one of our seats so the other seat was now open and that's how we scored seats on the next plane. But that meant we had to sit in the airport for another 11 hours. Okay, so we keep busy and we finally wound up getting on the plane almost a half a day later. Once we boarded, the plane ride was awesome, you know, meeting a bunch of people and stuff.

We're sitting on the plane and Cheese wakes me up, and he says, "Yo, bro, like we don't have a hotel." Now remember, inside this whole package deal there is supposed to be a hotel. Like hotel included, right? So I'm like, damn, like whatever. What a screw-up. Fuck!

We get to the airport in Hawaii, we get off the frickin' plane and I know we'll figure something out. I told Milla that Cheese had dropped the ball, and Milla said he had cash, and if we had to, we could always put it on his card. So we're looking at all these hotels trying to figure out what to do.

Cheese meets his boy, Buck, at the airport. One of the things we wanted to do was meet up with this dude, Greg Buckley, who was tight with Cheese. Buck was stationed in Hawaii, at one of the Oahu facilities, and Buck was going to show us around, show us a good time, you know?

Buck was an awesome dude. He was everything you'd expect a Marine to be. This is my shout-out to Buck! Rest in peace, bro.

Buck later became a Marine lance corporal and was stationed to some province in Afghanistan to train locals as part of the NATO withdrawal plan. Buck was 21 when he was murdered, along with two other Marines, after sharing a meal with an Afghan policeman who turned on them.

Buck picks us up from the airport, and he has to be back on base by a certain time. His superiors let him leave the base just because we were coming, so Buck picked us up, you know, and we we're thinking about pretty much sleeping on the beach.

We were going to all these hotels to find a room and we were told that a single night was $1,000 here or $800 there, $500 a night someplace else, you know, so I was kind of flipping out.

As we were asking around, I met this one guy; his name was Rich, and he worked at this hotel. He saw how stressed we were, and he said, "You know what? I'm going to let you get the suite for $150 a night." I said, "Dude, you're sold!"

And this is hotel is right on the beach. The cheapest room that night was $500 a night, $498, or something like that. Rich gave it to us for $150 a night. We were staying for eight nights, so that's $1,200 and I was freaking out. I'd already spent $600 on airfare to Hawaii (dumbass Cheese!) and cash was momentarily tight...which I'll explain in a moment. My parents were, like, "If we have to, you know what I mean, go ahead and get it just for two or three nights and then we'll switch out of it."

But it wound up being okay, we were good. We got the room, we threw our gear inside, stretched our legs...and then Cheese said he didn't want to pay, he wanted a personal room. I said, "What the fuck? How are you going to get a personal room? Oh, and everything is on my card, right? I just paid all my money and you told me we would have a hotel!" So he was pissed. He never even really paid me for that room. Which was fine, whatever.

We were on vacation and we brought $2,500 between us to enjoy ourselves, just to spend, because we thought the hotel was already paid for. That's the biggest part of it. But Cheese fucked that up.

When I'm going somewhere, I'm going to bring a set amount like $2,500, and Milla also brought $2,500. We always put our money together when we go out and I'm expecting Cheese to bring money and put it with ours. I'm expecting a flight with hotel included. So I'm bringing a set amount of money, I'm not coming out there with cash, straight cash. You know what I mean?

The reason why money was tight was because just before this trip, me and P-Money had to flush down a shit load of drugs. My cousin Chuck came to the Washington Street house one day, and he knocked on the door acting like he was the fucking police. We flushed almost everything! We had a lot of stuff in the attic we were trying to get down to flush, and P-Money is kneeling at the toilet flushing cocaine, just flushing, flushing, flushing, and I'm like, "Yo, bro, we got to get rid of everything!" He flushed down $12,000 of coke. And I'm just like, fuck! FUCK! You know what I mean? Like damn! And it was a fucking joke to my stupid-ass cousin because you just don't play like that, you know what I mean? Especially when he knew we got as mad as shit about crap like this. So that was big. This was right before Hawaii. This was the massive reason we didn't have any extra fucking money, man. We had to pay back A from our frickin' profits. Shit. Just shit.

Then on top of that we were hitting rock-bottom. We were partying Sunday to Sunday, you know what I mean? We were going out all the time...Sunday to Sunday. The money was going out as fast as it was coming in, and a lot of that money was going up our noses. I was getting tattoos literally once a week, going shopping, I had a girlfriend, we just hit Valentine's Day. There were a lot of expenses. There was no problem with money, we were making it left and right, but, dude, I'm not paying $1,000 a night for me to stay here and then also pay for these kids. Like now, to quote Muggs, "Good one, dude, what is this? A charity?" You know what I mean?

And besides, just because you have a bunch of money doesn't mean you have to spend it! The brokest people in the world are always the flyest people. You know what I mean? They spend all their money on material shit and go broke. And the richest people in the world, they don't need all that shit. They know what they have. You know? They can wear whatever, they know how much money they have in the bank, so they don't have to spend all that money.

Now that we're in Hawaii, me and Milla are hanging out together the whole time, and we're balling out. That was the crazy part of the story, like it wasn't about the room. I'm there for eight nights and no way I'm going to pay $1,000 a night. That's ridiculous. So we're going out, getting steak and eggs every morning. You know? We're going out to these boss restaurants. Me and Milla went out to every club on Waikiki Beach we possibly could. We hit happy hour every day, and we had fun, you know? Cheese didn't want to do anything, that clown was just sitting in the room.

Funny story, Cheese would wait until midnight to wake up, which is 5 o'clock back home, so, dude, how are you sleeping like that all day? Just so he could save money. He would get up and get a dollar McChicken or a dollar fry for McDonald's, you know, instead of getting up and eating breakfast with me and Milla. Cheese only spent $127.49. I'm telling you, eight days in Hawaii? Like, come on, man, like how the fuck do you do that?

But it's awesome, you know what I mean? We're hanging out with Buck, and he's taking us to the beach, we go surfing, well, they went surfing. I wasn't down to go surfing. There were no waves, you know what I mean? They were coming back with scrapes on their knees and elbows, but they went surfing. It was cool, the whole scene. We just had an all around good time.

So now the time is winding down, I'm pretty much ready to leave Hawaii. Truth is, I really didn't like Hawaii that much. I really didn't. Maybe it was because of the crew that I went with. You know, the year before I went with my Jew boys, Lucas and Corey, and we went to Miami, you know, and we balled out, we had a good time. And everything came out as planned, you know? The flight was good, nothing to worry about, we had an apartment to stay in, and so we had money to spend. You know? Then I go with these kids and everything felt just like, well, fucked up.

It's time to leave. The night before, we go to this dope restaurant, and Cheese, being the chef of our crew, he's the cook, he's the chef, we go to this boss restaurant, and Cheese orders a chicken picada off the kids' menu! So he can save money! It was $12.49. Me and Milla are getting filet mignon, we order a nice bottle of wine, you know what I mean? We're hanging out. Our last night in Hawaii, and like we're going home tomorrow so, you know, spend everything you got left. And when the bill comes, Cheese is like, "Well, I'm not paying any tax or any tip because I didn't get anything major like you guys." "You know, like, bro, you're sitting here, you're drinking our bottle of wine…" You hear what I'm saying? Guys don't do that. But whatever. We wound up paying the bill, but Cheese gave us $12.49. He pulled out a $10, two $1's, nine pennies and a couple of quarters. I swear. I couldn't believe it. He looked at us, and he said, "I'm Jewish." So I said, "Wow. All right, dude. I see how it is, bro, but whatever."

We're starting to leave the next morning. We're checking out of this hotel and we called Cheese's dad to check on our flights, and everything is good. "Yeah, everything is all set for you guys." We take him on his word and we checked out of the hotel. We're in a cab heading to the airport. Goodbye Hawaii. Suddenly we get a call from Cheese's dad. Now he says, "Oh, man!

You guys have to stay in the hotel one more night. The flights are canceled due to weather!"

What the fuck? You just told us...

We already checked out. We're fucked. He's like, "Well, damn! Well, you boys gotta get another hotel for the night." Damn, all right, whatever, dude. I call home and tell my parents we're stuck here another night.

Now we're looking for a hostel. We get to this hostel and there are these gay guys. "Hey, can I get you guys a room?" Yeah, well, we want a room. "We've only got one room left..." so we take it. And he's like, "Yeah, but there's only one bed in it." He smiled, looked at me and Milla, and he said, "Okay, you guys take the one bed, and your other partner can sleep on the floor." We're like, "No, dude, it's not working like that. We need two separate beds." So we wind up getting this room for 90 bucks for two nights and he's like, "You guys need your own sheets, and you also need your own towels. We don't supply those, you know." We get into this room and I'm like what the fuck? The room is in a shambles, there are all these nasty blood and cum stains on the mattresses and blankets, there's a bootleg air conditioning system, I have to share a bathroom with some cats I don't know, we have to share a kitchen, I'm like, "Yeah, dude, I gotta get out of here."

So I called home and told my mom she had to help us find a cheaper hotel by the airport, and we're just going to grab one of those for the night. So after some time went by, we got one of those. It was like the Treasure Cove Hotel, or Paradise Lodgings or some such nonsense...but it was a good cheap room so we took it. We're hoping it'll only be for one night and we'll get the hell out of Oahu before the tempest hits. Some sort of news about a big storm, wind warnings, cresting waves, hurricane-type weather, I don't know what the fuck, but I know we wanted to get home now before this shit starts happening.

Now it's about the bus. There is only one bus, of course, and it leaves every hour or so heading out to the airport. We have to catch this bus, right? We're sitting outside at some street-side tables by the ice cream store, eating ice cream. All the businesses around us are closing down because this storm is going to be hitting soon. Folks are putting plywood over their windows, placing sand bags by their doors...like it's going to get freaking ugly soon...and we see the bus. Here it comes! Cheese flags the bus. We get up, grab our gear, and we gun it over there. It's $10 to get on the bus. Me and Milla pay our $10 each, whatever. We sit down.

Cheese is standing there. He yells out, "Hey! I can't get on the bus!" I yell back, "What? Why can't you get on the bus?" "I don't have no money!" I'm like, "Bro, you just had cash!" "Nah, I don't have no money, man. You guys just go ahead. I'm just going to wait here until Buck gets out." I'm not going to do that to the kid. "Aw, come on, man, you're killing me!" I said. "Why don't you just get on the damn bus, bro?" So I paid his fare. Fuck. Whatever.

We get to the hotel by the airport and Cheese says, "Oh, I'm not staying in here. It's too small." I am...what? Like what? "Nah, I'm staying on the base with Buck. I don't have to pay nothing." I said, "Dude, you didn't even pay me for the last hotel! Now I've got a cheap one just for the night and we'll be out of here tomorrow. So if you don't want to stay here, fuck it, bro. Leave." Cheese wound up going to Buck's, whatever, at the Marine base. They wound up going out that night, Milla, Cheese, and Buck and his boys. I didn't go out. I stayed in the hotel. I pulled a 'Cheese'!

The next morning it's time to go. I'm ready to get the hell out of Hawaii, like let's move, you know? We get a late checkout at 1:00 p.m. Our flight leaves at 7:00 p.m. So I'm calling Cheese, calling Cheese, calling Cheese. "Like, dude, what time are you going to meet us at the airport?" Me and Milla are already there, waiting with our bags. Cheese says, "Yeah, the tickets should be there, Vic." So we check for our names at the ticket counter, and the tickets come up as 'Not found'. Now what the fuck?

There is nobody at the airport, and there were only two flights leaving on the announcement boards. The whole fucking terminal and airport is shutting down because of this incoming storm. Shit! Me and Milla were the only two people visible at the airport other than the people cleaning up in Starbucks. The only two people.

Like there was no one there! This is a major international airport! Unbelievable.

The boards said the only two flights were at 11:15 p.m. and 11:59 p.m. No 7:00 p.m. flight, no nothin'. I'm like, what?

I'm on the phone with Cheese and I tell him, "Cheese, call your dad. We don't have tickets, the flights ain't here, like we're fucked. We're stuck in Hawaii." Cheese says, "Nah, man, you don't know what you're talking about." His dad says, "Uh, well, you know, something got screwed up…"

Now I'm like fuck this, man. I call up my mom and dad and I go like, "I'm fucked. I'm fucking stuck in Hawaii with no tickets, nobody to talk to about it, no flights, no hotel, no cash, and this freaking storm is about to hit. I definitely need some help." They're like, "All right, whatever."

They called Cheese's dad, and Cheese's dad had turned his phone off, like he wouldn't answer our calls ever again, you know what I mean? I pretty much got beat out of my money even though I had a promissory note from Cheese. My parents were going to sue. They said they were going to sue this asshole over $600. They were so pissed. But the lawyer fees and court costs would have been way more than that, so they went fuck him, man. He's a scumbag.

So now I had to pay for another flight back home, and I had to leave Milla there on Oahu, because Milla told me to go ahead. That was Saturday, and we had class on Monday. We wouldn't have reached the mainland until late Sunday night and that would have just been to Arizona. And then we would still have to go from Arizona back to Providence on Monday, not arriving until early Tuesday if we were lucky. And we had class. So Milla goes, "Dude, go ahead and tell the professor I won't be there," because he and I had the same class. "Tell the professor our story." So I'm whatever.

I bought a one way ticket, and it was like $1,200. I board the freaking plane and I get out of Hawaii heading back home. Cheese took a first-class ticket back home the next day and Milla had to sit on the floor with three other people. They let these passengers sit on the floor because otherwise they would be stuck in Hawaii for another two weeks. It looked like all the flights out of Hawaii were locked down for the next two weeks.

I make it back to Providence late on Sunday night, but I didn't even go to class the next day. I woke up on Tuesday, I was so jetlagged. After we all got back home, Cheese wouldn't speak with me, you know? He was offended! Wow.

Chapter 12

Roofied on St. Patty's Day

And now it was work time. A hits me up. "Yo, you gotta make a trip." Boom-boom-boom. After class on the Tuesday I made it back from Hawaii, me and Turbs take down an address from A and we drive to New York City. We picked up a big shipment, threw it in the car and drove back. Business as usual. That's how it was week after week. Man, it was great to be home!

St. Patty's Day is rolling around, but this year it was different, it was a lot different in my sophomore year. Cheese, and all of us, were arguing a lot with our fraternity brothers, and we were like fuck these kids, and we just weren't really with it anymore. It was like everything had changed and this scene wasn't as cool as it had been. I'd changed a lot, you know? I was seeing a lot more, now that I had been dealing for over a year. It was like school didn't even matter, and the kind of stuff the fraternity was doing was so far from what I was now into. But we still had our connections with each other. Things weren't so far gone.

So I went out with my Washington Street crew, not with my fraternity brothers, you know what I mean? Everybody knew everybody, so it was like that was my crew on the side. I went out with my Washington guys, and we're all just killing it. It's us 30, plus the fraternity brothers, plus our sorority sisters, and we're all roaming the streets of Providence. It was really cool, knowing everybody on the street, no matter where I was. I wound up blacking out, and I was pissing on cars, and I also got hit by a car, not badly, but enough to spin me around. P-Money wound up carrying me, even though he was the same size as me, a little Italian dude from Brooklyn, carrying me on his back. He wound up dropping me, though. All his boys from Brooklyn were up, right?

I woke up, and that's when I got the call from Beth's mom. I don't remember much of it, but I answered the phone and I go like, "Who the fuck is this?"

Her mother was telling me that Beth was in trouble. She wanted me to help, do something. I said, "What the fuck happened?" Her mother said, "I don't know, but she is freaking out! I think she's been rufied! Please, Vic, find Beth and help her!" So I asked her mom where the fuck Beth was and her mom told me she was at a bar not far from where I was. Beth was at Finnegans.

P-Money says fuck it, bro, we've got to get this bitch out of there!" So we go to pick her up at Finnegans. We get in front of the Westin Hotel and that's right up the street from where my apartment was, and we just zip under the underpass. We get to the Westin and this girl is on the street fat butt ass naked. Beth is just fucking screaming, hollering, and everything else, man. She was hammered and she was all fucked up.

We get back to our apartment building and I thought Beth had her keys. So I'm like whatever. I'm hammered, too, so I'm thinking I'll just throw her in her apartment and I'm out; then I can go back out to drink and fight. Me and P-Money get Beth to her apartment.

I bring this chick all the way upstairs, and then we find out she had no keys! P-Money tells me to stay there with her and he'll be right back. "I'll be back to get you, Vic, don't worry about it, I'll be back." So, all right, I'm like fuck it, man. Me and Beth. Well, shit, we can't stay here in the hallway until P-Money returns, so I take Beth to my apartment. Big mistake.

When we get inside, this chick starts going off in my apartment. She started smashing bottles, pushing stuff off the counters onto the floor, wrecking the kitchen and the bathroom, and Beth was going freaking crazy. I took a video of Beth acting nuts so in case the cops came they would know exactly what happened and see I wasn't doing anything to her! I wasn't doing anything, it wasn't anything to do with me, I was just coming in! You know what I'm saying?

On top of that, I can barely stand up I'm so hammered, and I'm slurring my speech, my brain is on blink, right? And Beth is fried, too. She's cursing me out, screaming at me to go fuck myself, and things are quickly getting to a crescendo! The girl is freaking mad, like insane, unable to hear me or reason...her demons came out and they were throwing pitchforks! At me!

Suddenly Beth's friend, Sherry, comes running in. She's like, "Vic, I'm so sorry, Beth is so fucked up...Beth, Vic is trying to help you, Hon! He's trying to help you!"

That's when Beth explodes, getting it into her head that I'm fucking Sherry. Shit! "Fuck you! Fuck you, you bastard! I know you're fucking Sherry!" Beth ran at Sherry with the broken bottle trying to kill her. And that was her best friend. I'm like, yo! What the fuck!

So we had to lock Beth in my room, and I told Sherry, get out of here! I don't care what you do, but do not call the police, I have too many drugs in my apartment, plus I'm growing weed so I don't want them in here. She's like, "Fuck it, Vic! I already called the cops." I'm like, "Yeah, you're fucking retarded, man!"

The phone is ringing, and it's the cops...Sherry must have given them my number. I'm ignoring the calls, and then I call my two boys, Kev and Louis, and they come through and are just watching everything, like being my witnesses, you know? All of a sudden the cops bust into my apartment, like out of nowhere!

They came in, and slammed me on the couch. "Why the fuck didn't you answer our calls? What the fuck are you doing to this girl?" There's a bunch of broken glass in my apartment thanks to Beth's craziness, and Beth's feet are bleeding because she was stomping on the glass. Her feet! It was crazy! So I'm like, "Dude, her feet are bleeding! I'm hammered, Dude, her feet are bleeding! I didn't touch this girl! Like, she's in my apartment! Like, what are you doing?"

They let me up, and I took off, and I got out. Now my boys are still in there and they were saying, "Yo, Vic, where are you going?" So I said, "Bro, I have to get out of here! Just watch out for that plant, watch out for that plant!" I knew the cops weren't going to find the other drugs that were stashed away on the roof; I had like a whole rooftop apartment and my drugs were all stashed, so I told them to watch out for my plant, man. The cops heard me and they said, "Oh, yeah?" And so they fucking poured bleach all over my plant. I was next door, across the street in my neighbor's house, and my boys told me to come back, that everything was good. My whole place was a fucking wreck. The cops wound up taking Beth to the hospital. It was crazy stuff. That was just like, whoa!

My plant, man. It had just started budding and I was able to pull weed off it any time I wanted. I had about two pounds of bud on that plant. Yeah, so I was looking forward to that, but the bastards poured bleach on it, and they killed it, and I never got to fuck with that plant. Beth wound up paying me back for the lost shit but, you know, whatever. I'm not going to fuck with that.

Now was when I started really getting deep with Beth's friends. I met her best friend, Paige. Paige was a slinky fox...she had it going on! Long and lean, she was gorgeous with a beautiful smile and big round eyes. I wondered about her. One time I was in Beth's apartment and I took Paige's bottle of wine. I opened it, liked it, and fucking finished it. Beth was like, "Vic! That's Paige's!" So Paige is like, "Well, damn! Beth is a crazy bitch... Vic's hot...I'll try to fuck Vic. Beth is the easy way to that." So Paige asked Beth one day, "Like, oh, I need Vic's number, Beth. Remember when he took my bottle of wine? He has to pay me back."

So now me and Paige start hanging out. I told you Beth and I lived in the same apartment building, and my apartment was above hers, so now I'm fucking her friend right upstairs, right above my girlfriend's apartment...while she's in there! It was hot! It was awesome, you know what I mean? I wanted to fuck Paige when I knew Beth was downstairs. That made it even hotter. It got pretty crazy.

The three bedroom apartment I was in was now all mine. The reason I had my own apartment was that I had moved in with my boys, Chowder and Nick. Chowder wound up leaving school; he couldn't handle it. He was getting fat and nasty, and he was a Mommy's and Daddy's boy, so he had to go back home. And Nick, he lived in Rhode Island, and his dad's the president architect of Johnson and Wales. His family was chill, you know, so Nick didn't really want to live in the apartment anymore. He wanted to live in his house back home, kind of around the corner, so he moved out. Nick would come by occasionally to take care of my plant. Before the cops killed it.

At this point I'm fucking all of Beth's friends. It was a great ride, I'm telling you. Beth had some good-looking friends, and most of them wound up in my bed. Beth was pledging her sorority and just got in, whatever, and we're having a good time. Me more than most.

Alumni weekend rolls around; sophomore year is quickly coming to an end. A is up for the festivities, along with his henchmen Dappa and Fat Boy; Money Mike is winging for them. Everybody is ready for a good time, along with the Washington Street crew. On Friday, all the alumni are just arriving, so we gather and go out to Olives and Club Pearl for the night. On Saturday morning you wake up, and then, for the entire day, there is a block party.

We shut down a place called Rick's Roadhouse out on Richmond Street; they have ribs, steaks, "Wings from Hell", everything. And every alumnus is there! It's freaking awesome. We're killing it, you know, we're all partying and getting hammered. When we pull up, we come in, and I'm showing the three felons, A and all his guys. A's like, "Yo, Slicktor Victor, introduce us to all these joints. Introduce us to all these girls." You know, the girls just love me, and they're going like, "Oh, Vic, who are your friends? These guys are cool," and whatever. They don't even know these guys are felons!

Chapter 13

Money Mike's Turn

I got roofied, man. I got fucking roofied.

My girl, Brookie P, was serving. She was our bartender. There were so many people at the bar, and there were pitchers, lots of pitchers. Pitchers and pitchers of margaritas. The pitchers weren't getting cleaned or something. But there was this old creepy man, this really creepy man at the bar. He was the only old man there. Gay Ray. He looked like something out of a nightmare; he was short with gray hair and a freaking creepy face.

I remember driving because I had Money Mike's keys, but we couldn't find Money Mike anywhere. Later on we found out that MM was getting mobbed in his drawers. That means he was getting raped by Gay Ray. Or whatever the hell was going on.

Money Mike was this really good-looking rich white kid who drove the felons around. I told you he had a square jaw, a handsome forehead, good features…kind of like some kid you'd think should be a crew member on a World Cup sailing ship.

So on that Saturday night, on alumni weekend, Money Mike was drinking and drugging or whatever, and he got separated from our crew, and started walking toward the Washington Street house. I guess he didn't know that instead we're all heading downtown for the night. We lose this kid, and we're calling and texting him, but no response. We don't think anything of it. I've passed out, so the crew drops me off at my apartment, and the kids brought me upstairs. I'm not waking up until the next morning, and when I do, I wake up in Beth's apartment. I had chills, my face was pale as a ghost, and I knew I got roofied. I know the deal.

I wake up at eight. Beth's like, "Yo, Baby, A and all his guys are upstairs in your apartment. I let them in." I said, "What the fuck?" She said, "Yeah, they have something to tell you." So I go upstairs to see what's up; my head feels like the inside of a carburetor. They're like, "Yo, Money Mike got mobbed in his drawers last night. Like, wake up, Vic, we've got to go back to Washington Street. Get up, get up, get up!" I'm like, what the fuck?

We get back to the Washington Street house, and that's when we all hear the story. Pretty much, this kid was walking on the side of the road, and this old man picked him up and, like, was doing whatever he was doing with him. A got a call from Money Mike's phone, and when A took the call, there was this old man's voice. It was like, "Hey, yeah, come pick this kid up; I'm all done with him. We're at Cheaters Strip Club on Allens Avenue. Come pick him up."

They go pick him up, P-Money, A, and Turbs, and Gay Ray said, "Give him this sweatshirt when he wakes up. He won't remember me but he'll remember the sweatshirt," and there were a bunch of cum stains on the sweatshirt. It was disgusting, a bunch of shameful things.

The old man was like, "Yeah, I had a good time with him," and Gay Ray was rinsing out his mouth and shit. The kid, Money Mike, woke up later in the morning and he's like, "Bro, I was so fucked up last night, but I remember getting the craziest blow job of my life!" He said, "I was definitely fucking the shit out of this girl, man," and they're like, "Dude, you were with Gay Ray!" And he was like, "Nah, man, I was definitely fucking this chick. She was a blondie, and…" "No, bro, you were with a dude!" They showed him the hoodie and told him what Gay Ray said, and this kid tried to kill himself on the spot. In the Washington house. We had to chase this kid down, grab him and shit, make sure he was all right, you know? It was fucked up. Yeah, that was pretty much alumni weekend that year. That was a massive story. That was crazy.

After that, it was time for formal. We didn't have a formal that year but we had other plans in mind. I was automatically going with Beth. But the thing is, I didn't really want to go with her. We were just fuck buddies, you know? I wasn't really trying to let everyone in the world know. Nobody even knew I was fucking her except certain people. You know, I just wanted to keep my stuff on the low so I could still do whatever I wanted.

And one of my bros said, "Yeah, Vic, are you really going to go to the formal with Beth?" I'm like, "Yeah, I'm going to go with Beth." So all right, cool. Whatever.

The thing is, we were going to a formal back in the Poconos. SDT, who were my sorority sisters, had their formal last year in the Poconos, and I had brought them to my house. I also got them a hook-up in this hotel I used to work at called the Great Wolf Lodge; it's an indoor water resort and kind of cool. Last year they paid $500 and got 15 rooms for three nights. They had food, too, and everything was covered. I used to work there, and the hotel crew was my friends and shit, so I worked this deal and it was awesome. And then I also had an indoor pool at this huge house that my grandparents built for us, so last year was a pretty outrageous formal weekend. Now the Phi Sigs, which was Beth's sorority, they also want to come and get the same deal, you know?

They're like, "Oh, Vic, we want to go there," whatever, so I'm like, "Alright, cool. I'll see what I can do; maybe I can hook you up." So I got it worked out, and now I'm going with Beth to this formal back in the Poconos.

I get all coked-up the night before we're supposed to leave, and Beth comes into my apartment drunk and she's fucking with me. You know what I mean? I think this was all kind of planned, and it was really kind of weird. What I think is she didn't really want all these girls coming to my house. You know how that goes. Somebody sees you've got this or you've got that, and they're going to try to come at you, so, yeah. So Beth was kind of acting funny.

Me, P-Money, Turbs and Muggs are doing some coke, and Beth comes upstairs. "Oh," she says, "do you want me to pack your bag?" I said, "No, Beth, I've got it all done. Don't worry about it."

Beth's all drunk and fucked up like she was that one time on St. Patty's Day, and I'm like, "You have to get the fuck out of here, like, we're doing business here, we've got a bunch of coke in here, you just have to stop."

But this chick just comes in and throws beer in our faces. Fucking bitch! Then she started slapping the shit out of me, in my apartment! The guys start bugging out. I'm like "Get the fuck out of my apartment right now, Beth." I poured beer on her head, I throw her keys down the stairs, and she starts slapping me and shit, so I literally pushed her out the door with my forearms, like just moving her out very slowly, so no one gets hurt... "Beth, get the fuck out. Get the fuck out, Beth. You have to leave now, Beth …"

She made this big, huge antic slip in the fucking hallway. So now the neighbors come pouring out to see what the hell is going on, and they are going like, "This girl's fucking crazy, Buddy! You need to leave her alone!" I go back into my apartment and I'm packing up all our coke and shit because I can feel like something is about to go down. Beth's probably going to call the cops, and we have to get the fuck out of here.

We packed up all the shit, whatever, and I went back to Beth's apartment. I'm knocking on the bitch's door, like "Yo, are we going, or whatever?" So Beth texts me, "I'm not going with you. I'm going with someone else." I'm okay, all right, whatever.

I went to sleep and I woke up the next morning. I was going to hit it off in the morning and she tells me I should have called her early in the morning because she's already left and is now just about arriving there, in the Poconos. I said, "I thought you were leaving at 11:00 a.m.," and she said, "No, we already left."

I'm like, alright, fuck it. So now I know I'm not going to formal. I'm heartbroken. Her friend, Paige, the girl I was fucking with upstairs in my apartment, she's like, "Yo, Vic, yo! Beth is going with this other kid. Like, it's nothing serious between them, or anything at all; I don't even know why she's going with him." I said, "I ain't worried about it." So Paige says, "Why don't you surprise her and come with me? That will really piss her off." I'm like, "Paige, we can't do that. I'm not doing that."

So I called Milhem, and I go up to Milhem's house for the weekend with Cheese, and we hang out up there. Then Beth is hitting me up the entire time she's at this formal, you know what I mean? "I don't even want to be with this kid!" she says. You know? "He hit me and now he's sleeping with another girl, they're on the floor. I really don't like these guys…" And whatever, whatever. I'm like, "Yo, have fun, man." Pretty much just leave me fucking alone. Beth.

But at that point, I kind of felt like, damn. I went through all of this shit with this girl this year, you know what I mean? I just need to wife it up, I thought. It made me feel sort of hurt, that I didn't get to go to that formal, and I was kind of pissed about that. Like it's not like she just went by herself; she actually took somebody else. I mean, man, that's crazy. So, whatever. Oh, yeah, and I had just gone shopping with Beth a few days before and we got her all her formal stuff…so now she's wearing all this new stuff for some other dude, you know what I mean? I'm like, fuck it.

Beth got back from the formal, and I was like yo, like, we have to start dating. You know what I mean? I might just as well put the title on it. So we wound up doing that, and it was all good. And I said, yeah, fuck it, that's what we're going to do. I mean, we've got to get out of here, we've got to move to Miami. 'Cause I can't be dating you still living in Providence, and you know you can't date me while I'm living in Providence, and I'm developing too much shit, and I've got to get out of here. So she's like, whatever, I'm down. Let's go to Miami.

So we go to Miami. We move away, and that was that.

Chapter 14

The Summer Before Miami

But first I lived in New Hampshire for the whole summer with Beth. That was just a fucked-up crazy experience. There was a lot going on there. It wasn't really my taste for the woods, you know? It was different. I'm not used to going to a town where there's only like 1,000 people living in the fucking town. You know what I mean? What kind of shit is that? You know?

Even so, it was a very relaxing summer. I was able to detox a little bit, except I was smoking a bunch of weed. Just to cope through it. I wound up hanging out, working in her parents' bagel shop up there. They were a very dysfunctional family, but what family isn't? There is no perfect family…but hers was very dysfunctional.

On my last night in Providence, I was with all my boys. P-Money, Dray, my cousin Chuck, and Wi-Fi, and they were all going to stay in my apartment, the one above Beth's old place. We smoked a bunch of weed and got hammered and shit, and then my flight left. I met my dad in the airport, in Miami. We brought all my stuff to Miami, and we stayed for like a week, got things organized, and then I headed out to New Hampshire for the summer.

It's a lot of stuff, man, a lot of stuff. That was a big year. The felon, A, he goes down that summer, after I moved to Miami, while I was in New Hampshire. He wound up getting arrested so everything seriously started shutting down. I got out of that scene just in time, like my angels were watching over me, man. It was like no more drug running. There was none of that shit any more. Everything was done. All that money we had and everything, all of that shit was just gone, man, just gone.

Just as well, because we had all started doing too much of those drugs and we didn't want to let like A and Dappa and those kids know we were using our own shit so much because that's bad business. When you do some of it, yeah, you can come back with your money, but when you start getting heavy into the drug game, the suppliers are not going to trust someone who's doing the product. You know what I mean? Because they're going to think you're skimping them out. But no, we always had our shit, but that was the thing, that was where the money was going, it was going up our fucking noses, man. We were blowing a lot of product. We were our own best customers.

We had thousands of dollars, all the time, and we always went out to clubs, like this place Monet. We'd go to Monet every Friday and we always got VIP'd. At that time we went to Monet and made it very epic, you know, A, and all of them, came out with us, so we're deep as hell, we've got a bunch of chicks with us, and you got me, Cheese, Milla, P-Money, Turbs, and A. Oh, And Muggs. That right there, you're talking about five grand apiece, pretty much, and you got this dude, Devin Price, that's my boy, too, but you got him and his boys, I mean like they're laying down five grand apiece so we're just competing, we're doing bottles, and rich bitches, coming out VIP with bitches going in, we're just having fun, you know what I mean? The girls, they make it a real competition, but whatever, we're having fun, you know? We put down $20,000 a night, with all of us putting our money together. We had an awesome time!

Do I miss this life? No, I've talked about it with my buddies, and no, I don't. It was very hectic, it was very stressful, and it was cool to have all that money, but I'd just rather sit down and work for my shit now without looking over my back every two seconds, you know? It was bad! Providence was easy because Providence is one of the most under-the-radar cities in the world. And cops are a lot more corrupt in Providence. I wasn't really worried about the cop thing, but when you have to worry about kids dying, overdosing, you know? You don't know what these kids are putting in their bodies before you sell them the stuff.

It was a fun lifestyle. It was definitely fun. I could do it again, it was easy, but if I did it now, with the mindset I have now, I would be a lot smarter. I wouldn't be spending all of that money. I would make just enough to invest in something actual, legal, you know what I'm saying? I would make $20,000, and of that I'd invest $10k, and I would have the other $10k that was just building. That's how I would do it now.

Junior Year

Chapter 15

A Piece of Me

While I was spending the summer in New Hampshire, Beth's family took me and Beth out for dinner one night. Her family was kind of like trying to show off, trying to show me and Beth a good time and stuff, and we wound up going out to a local somewhat expensive dinner house. There were all these bottles of wine, and massive steaks, and everything, and I'm, well, okay, cool. They got it like that? Okay, then...okay! Perfect.

So then the bill comes and you could see their eyes just pop out of their heads, like they'd never seen a bill this big before. You know? Just trying to show off too much and it bit them in the ass, pretty much. So that's when I pulled out my card, you know, being very funny while they were looking at the bill and I kind of like snagged the check out of her mom's hands and handed my card and the check to the waiter and paid for everything. It was about a $2,000 bill.

It was pretty funny. But they didn't think so. They didn't really like me too much after that. I did it out of respect because I knew they didn't have it, and I saw they were in pain, and trying to negotiate things, and I said, whatever, I have it. Here it is. So I paid for it. And like I said, after that, things started turning around. They weren't really talking to me, and they weren't very sociable with me. Wow. Why did they have to be like that? They just didn't look at me the same, so I packed up my stuff and I wound up going back.

I went to Providence because we were moving to Miami in a week anyway, and I got into this big brawl. My sorority sisters are having this huge party before the beginning of the year and I'm there drinking, having a good time, when one of my sorority sisters comes up to me and says, "Vic, you need to get out of here! Like I just heard that the Phi Sigma Phi brothers are going to jump you!" And I'm like, cool!

I turn up the music, and there's me and my buddy, Jimmy, and we're walking around the party, and I want to know who wants to fight me. You know? "Who wants to fight? I'll fight every one of you one-on-one right now! C'mon! Do you want to fight? How about you, Guido?"

As I'm walking around, there's this little Asian kid in the corner who I used to pick on a little bit in orientation and during freshman year, in a fun way, you know, not meaning any harm but teasing-like, and the PSP brothers were over there amping him up. They were like pouring beers over his head, they were ragging-around like a pit bull, gettin' him amped up. They were acting like Floyd Maywether against

Pacquiao. This kid was the same height and same size as me, you know.

So they wind up throwing this kid at me, and we wound up brawling. After a few moments I wound up clipping this kid by the back of his leg and smashing a bottle over his head. He got back up from the bottle smash, and he's bleeding everywhere. It was like a murder scene. And I just hit him with a two-piece, a jab and an uppercut, and I put him in a headlock and took him to the ground. And I told everybody, you know, "Back the hell away from me, or I'll kill this kid!" You know, the whole fraternity is trying to jump on me, so the kid tapped out and he's like, "Vic, please, let go!"

I let go of him and get up and the whole fraternity swarms at me. But Milla is with me as everybody is coming at me, and I yelled, "Milla, you got my back? You got me? You got me?" And he's like, "Yeah, Vic, I got you. Don't worry about it!" So I started fighting and everything, and Milla and I wound up taking off, out the door and down the street.

I ran for a bit and then stopped and let them catch me because I wanted to give them a few more broken teeth and bloody noses. They were beating on me and Milla, but didn't do any damage. I left the fight with not one scar except a little cut on my finger from some broken glass. My friend, Lucas, who was with me in Miami, and my girl, Alex, from freshman year, pulls up in his car. You know, they whip around and pick us up. Milla and I jump in and we head out to get Serge, which is the bodyguard of our group. Serge is the big muscular guy who could bench press 580 pounds… He was only 5'9", but he was an animal. He played the role of security and sometimes put the beat on a few kids for me when I was in a pickle or two…like always. Serge was the muscle of our Washington Street crew. For sure, you didn't want to mess with him.

So we're on our way to get Serge, but there are a bunch of guys from the fraternity following us in their car. There was a fork in the road, and Lucas swerved left and then jukes back right and they wind up trying to do the same thing and crash into a pole! It was crazy! So we get Serge, but we're safe now, at least for a little while.

The next day my crew and I wind up fighting again. We wound up fighting some other crowd that night, but whatever, and then I went to Miami the next day. Me and Beth are at the airport, we're on the plane, and we get to Miami. It was cool, you know. We're enrolling in school, we're going to this new campus, and we're checking out what we have to wear because at this Miami campus we have to dress up for classes, so it was kind of weird, it was kind of "Wow, like what's going on?"

Chapter 16

Living in Magic City

It was totally different at the Miami campus. In Providence, the professors wouldn't give two fucks about you, you know? I was even told it was going to be like that; everyone knew that JWU Prov was like being thrown to the sharks.

The Miami campus was very small; there were like 2,200 kids at the whole campus, kind of like a middle-sized high school, while Providence had 3,000 kids just in my class alone. It was 12,000 kids versus 2,000...a big difference! It was kind of weird, you know, because we had to dress up every day, with a suit and tie. That was your attire. I learned a lot more at the Miami campus. I was able to put my mind to work, along with the minds of others, who, it turns out, didn't really know as much as me, you know? That was the good thing about it. I stood out in all my classes.

I met a lot of cool kids, too. It was a diverse campus, so that was good...lots of different types of people. I didn't really like them all, but that was okay; I didn't have to. It was pretty much an all-black kind of campus, you know? It wasn't really my scene, and it wasn't like an actual big campus. It was like one building, one long-assed building with everything connected to it, and that was kind of shitty.

I had to pick my concentration that year, and I chose Concerts and Events. My department threw a concert that year and I had a couple of lead roles and stuff like that. I wound up leaving that campus being very, very popular without doing much, you know, just being that face, being that fly guy. I was just killing it, you know? And I found that to be awesome.

My professors at Johnson and Wales, Miami, were great. They knew a lot of stuff and actually taught you. I had this one professor, Professor Chang. I suck at math, absolutely suck at math, but he got my math skills up from the bottom level to where they are now, which is near top notch. You know what I mean? Like this man worked with me on every little thing, and he gave a lot of his time. Like I would still be taking a test, and he wouldn't leave until I figured out the last problem. He wanted me to figure everything out, so he would break it down for me right there, on the spot, until I could figure it out. He would make it so clear it was almost like he would put the answer in my face. We had this crazy connection. He was definitely a traveling man, if you get what I mean. He was a Freemason kind of guy, and we had a connection through that, so that was kind of cool.

And then there was Professor Skilling, definitely a cool down to earth guy. I still think to this day he was having sex with some of the college girls, but whatever, he was a cool hip dude, you know what I mean? Very into sports. He would give us free tickets to the Miami

Heat games, him and Professor Andre. Andre was another professor in the Hospitality Department, and I took a class with her, and she was cool, and I hung out with these professors a lot. They were good people, and they were good to me.

As for the kids, my best friend was Josh, and we were like identical almost. We hit it off from Day One, you know what I mean? We still talk today, he's like my buddy, and we used to hang out smoking all types of weed. He was showing me around, and soon Miami was like my own backyard.

One of my buddies, Drew, is out there from Providence. I called him Drewstein. He also transferred to the Miami campus. And then there were Beth's friends, Bethany and this girl Anna S. Anna was from Rhode Island, and she went to JWU Prov with us, and now she's at JWU Miami, too.

And another one of Beth's friends, Stacy, she's also here. Stacy was one of Beth's best friends, and I had already had sex with her. I had told Beth about it during the summer, so it was kind of awkward with Stacy out here, you know? Beth didn't want to say anything to her, but she was definitely pissed at Stacy for having sex with me. So we're all hanging out, having a good time, and it was great to have kids we knew from home around us.

Like I said, Anna was friends with Beth and she would take Beth out with that girl Bethany, who was a 'hood-ass bitch from Georgia, and they would text me like, "Yeah, Vic, like you're seeing other girls." They knew I was cheating on Beth, but they made it easier for me, you know? They were helping me cheat on their friend, Beth, because they were hitting me up, like, "Yeah, we're not coming home yet, you know what I mean? You can be cool and chill now, whatever, and we'll text you on the way home, Vic. We'll text you when we're on our way!" And they would hit me up and tell me their ETA when they were coming home, and when to have the chick I was banging out of the apartment and all that kind of good stuff. So, yeah.

I also hung out with these other girls. When me and Drew would hang out, we hung out with Chelsea, Jill, and Emily. I told you I wound up having sex with Emily because she went to high school with Millham. So me and Drew, he was a big part of my junior year, and we would hang out, and he was with me all the time. Drew was trying to get with Jill, and also with Chelsea, but he never did, though I wound up fucking Emily. Oh, man, Emily. Nice straw-gold hair and pretty shoulders. She was sweet to me in bed, you know what I mean?

Drew and me would hang out with Chelsea and Jill, just two cool girls from Massachusetts. It was like staying in your comfort zone with your friends, you know, just meeting all kinds of kids, and hanging out. The beach, the fun, and my sister came down to visit a couple of times...it was just an overall good time, you know?

And there was my buddy, Sean, from down the hall. When I first moved to Miami, I met this guy in the elevator, and I could just tell he wasn't, you know, a Miami down-South country guy. He had New York swag, so I asked him where he was from, and he was from Harlem. We were talking and it turned out I kind of knew the cat. He was related to my best friend from home, and later I went to school at Prov with this kid and everything. There was my boy, Kev, who I got my weed and shit from a lot of times, in sophomore year, in junior year, senior year, and Kev was Sean's Godbrother. So this guy is living down the hall from me and his Godbrother is like my boy from home! I called my buddy Kev on the phone, and he's like, "Yeah, yeah, link up with him. Sean is going to look out for you," so I hung out with Sean a lot. He got me my first job at the Soho Hotel, and we still talk today. Sean was like 30 years old at the time. When I first arrived in Miami he would show us around, take us to spots, get us into different kinds of bars and clubs. It was cool.

This was also the year me and most of my crew turned 21, and we went to Atlantic City. It was me, Muggs, P-Money, and there were about 40 of us who went there. We met Ray J, the big rap artist and songwriter, and we went out to this one club and Muggs got us on the stage, and it was just a great time. It was all of us, and we were all Capricorns. Me, P-Money, Muggs, and

Milla. We're all born just a few days after each other. I'm born first, I'm the 24th, Muggs is the 27th, and P-Money and Milla are both born on the 28th of December. So us four were hanging out, and we have all of our friends from home, and we booked out a bunch of rooms at Caesar's Palace and we just balled out and had a great time. You know what I mean? We did a lot of drugs, and stuff like that, and that was for my birthday, which is also when Beth bought me a python.

Another friend I had was Anna L, and she was a great friend. Anna was Dominican, and she lived in Miami. I would hang out with her all the time! That's my girl, I love her to death, and she's my best girlfriend; she taught me all my Spanish, she and my barber.

Now that we're in Miami, we're hitting the beach. It was me and Beth, and we're going to the beach and doing all these cool things like hanging out at restaurants, going shopping, enjoying the palm tree life, you know?

We had just got to Miami and were settling into our apartment, getting ready for the new school year, when Beth's family comes down to check things out and drop off a car for us. I'm paying for the apartment, and it's like a one-way situation, you know? Beth doesn't have to pay for anything.

Her mom and stepdad get into town and they deliver this car, and we do whatever we have to do like get new license plates, and her folks wanted to hang out. I was just with her family the whole summer, and remember, they started turning on me a little bit at the end, over that restaurant check, so I hung out with them the first night they got there, and I made nice.

The next day I told them I was going out with my friends. I told Beth to bring some of her girlfriends over to hang out with her parents. And they got a little angry about that. They were offended, see? The poor bastards were indignant. It's always the ones who accuse others of being insulting when they're the ones that started it! Give me a fucking break. Fucking meatheads.

Now they up the ante because when I got back home from class, they had bought a whole bunch of food and stuff like that for my apartment…but it was just for Beth, nothing for me. They didn't give me a thing, in my own house. You know what I mean? So that was kind of shady. And that's when I stopped liking her parents. Here I am, paying the rent, the utilities, the freaking gas for the freaking car, nights out on the town…Beth is paying nothing…and these adult babies are treating me this way?

As the months drew on, I hit up her parents. I said, "You know what? Listen, I'm paying $1,500 a month, and I think it would only be right if I see at least a dollar from you. How about every month, you guys give me $50? Just so you're kicking in something for Beth."

They told me, "Well, we don't have $50 a month. But Vic, what we can do is we're going to get Beth into the dorm so you don't have to worry about her staying there with you. How about that?" Me and her mom wound up getting into an argument, along with me and her stepdad, and me and her real dad. I wound up cursing them all out. Like fuck you!

They shut off her credit cards and everything and told Beth she was out here on her own, and to let that little bastard take care of you. You know? So, whatever. So I'm taking care of this girl, and Beth and I decide to tough it out because we had serious feelings for each other, you know? Like we're in this thing together and we want to make it work out, and so fuck them, fuck her parents, and we'll do this on our own. It was serious, man. They drove us tighter, you know?

And it was good with Beth. Just me and Beth, man. Sleeping by the beach, you know? Nights like that, we would just do fun stuff, lovey-dovey stuff, and I'm not a lovey-dovey guy, you know what I mean? Do you know the joys of being with one woman, a woman you've committed to, and who is committed to you? It's absolutely fucking amazing, man. There's like this energy that links you, and it has a power over you, and it just connects you in your heart. I felt it, and Beth did, too, and it kind of took us over…and in the daytime when we were apart, I missed her in my arms, the sweetness of her, the fragrance of her skin, the honey of her lips…and at night I could bring her deep within my spirit and caress her through the long soft nights, and dream with her as we drifted through the warm darkness. That was special, man. This was one of the joys of being alive and loving my girl.

But sooner or later everything changes.

Beth finally landed a job, and she's working like two days a week at a juice bar making about 70 bucks every two weeks, something dumb like that. I wasn't going to take it from her, of course; she could keep her money. We were going out on nice dates and everything, and while she was working those couple of days, I started hanging out with her friend, Stacy, behind her back. This was the girl I'd told Beth about during the summer, that we'd hooked up before. You know, so Beth's at work and I go pick up Stacy, bring Stacy over to the apartment, bang her for a few hours until Beth gets out, then take Stacy home. I had another girl out here, too, Emily. I told you I met Emily through Milhem; Emily had gone to high school with Milhem back in Massachusetts, so I hung out with her, you know. I fucked Emily; I fucked Stacy; and I would also just hang out at the barber shop next door.

I remember this one time I got this girl's number right in front of Beth, it actually happened two times, and like it was a Spanish girl, and I'm speaking Spanish, and Beth has no clue what's going on, you know? These chicks are hitting on me, and so I'm taking these girls up and down.

I didn't like always being around Beth, you know, 'cause when you're around someone too much, it's like nothing fun or new or exciting is going to come of it because you see each other too much.

Anyway, Halloween rolls around. It's just me and Drewstein this year, and we got dressed up like Pauly D and Vinny from the Jersey Shore, which was really big back then. We went out to South Beach, and we killed it. It was a great Halloween and mind you, it was the only Halloween when nothing bad happened.

Chapter 17

Making Magic

It's getting close to Thanksgiving and I was working at the Soho Beach House Hotel on Collins Avenue, thanks to Sean who got me this job. The Soho is like for royalty, and all the celebrities go there. It's a membership-only hotel and I'm seeing celebrities all day. I wound up getting a side job with this guy who was a paparazzi. One day Dennis Rodman is there, another day a rap artist named Talib Kweli from Brooklyn is there, and I'm thinking, like, wow, I can get paid for spotting these guys. This paparazzi was telling me like how a single photo of Tom Cruise or Brad Pitt is worth more than what some movie directors make for shooting a film, so my eyebrows went up, and I started calling him and informing him when people were there. So that was kind of fun working with paparazzi for a little bit and I made some good cash.

It's Thanksgiving week, and I can't go home for Thanksgiving. My parents send a bunch of food down to me, but it gets trapped in the mail and I don't ever get it. I'm sitting in Miami by myself, and I've got to work 18 hours a day the whole freaking week. It was crazy. But I had a good time anyway because I was at a bunch of private parties. P. Diddy and Jennifer Lopez had a private party that week, so it was definitely a great time, and a great place to work at.

I was the inside security guard. I'm pretty much running that building, like members have to show me their member's card to come inside the building. The celebrities I met there were Paris Hilton, Talib Kweli, Russell Simmons, Kanye West, Jay-Z, Katy Perry, Rose Smith, Jessica Simpson, Justin Timberlake, and Amanda Seyfried. All in the short time I'm working there. I worked there for about five months. I was working the party, and by the time I got off at, what? 11 o'clock at night, the party was just getting started.

I was at work, and like I said, it was membership only. The management wanted all of us to wear specific clothing. I was dressing in their stuff but putting it into my own style, you know? I was connecting with the members, who were the celebrities, and the management didn't like that. They didn't want you getting close to the members. You're not supposed to speak to them. Your phone is not supposed to be out, either, because you might be taking photos or some shit. I already had a strike against me for texting on the job, and they were also bitching and complaining about the shoes I was wearing. I had these funny looking moccasins and everyone was loving them, so I kept wearing them. Even though they told me not to wear them again, I still wore them, whatever. I got to arguing with the tight-ass lady supervisor and before she could fire me, I told her, you know what? I'm just going to leave. And that's it. I didn't need their bullshit with this job, you know? It's a lot of bullshit. I'd been at this job for three months, and it's just a lot of bullshit, so I left that job.

Beth's back from break by this time, and now I have to find money somehow. I meet up with my barber next door, and me and him, you know, we're selling drugs. I'm buying weed off him, and stuff like that, and I would make a couple of sales for him here and there, you know what I mean? He would pay me back with mounds of money. He didn't even care.

He would give me ounces of weed to sell to people, and these would be like my friends and some of the kids on campus. I would go to the barbershop, get a haircut, and pick up the weed for my friends. I would always come back and bring the money to the barber. The last three or four times he didn't even ask for the money back. He just let me keep all of it; it was like 300 bucks for an ounce and it was like four ounces, so… He let me keep all the money. It was cool.

It was my barber who introduced me to the Russian mob. I met the Russian mob in Miami. I started speaking a little Russian, you know? I had some interesting moments over there hanging out with them. They showed me some crazy stuff. That really opened my eyes. Like, wow, man, my boys, we were running shit in Prov, you know, as far as the drugs went, but it was nothing near the operation I saw these actual boss dudes had going on. You know what I mean? The Russians and the Ukrainians? That was amazing!

I saw the international drug trade, and shit; it was fucking amazing! Like how everything was organized, and how the strippers were the mules for the shit. Huge amounts of drugs, huge amounts of money, huge amounts of weaponry, but more so the quality of clientele they had. You know what I mean? I'm talking about like you've got people you send the shit to in the UK, and then you're sending the shit to Germany, and then you're sending the shit back to Russia and the Ukraine, and then everywhere in the United States, and you're fucking killing the game. And then you have strip clubs all around, you know what I mean, all around town, to really hide all of that shit…it's crazy!

They were running all kinds of shit, but mostly what I saw was cocaine and ecstasy.

Ecstasy can be dangerous because it has multiple ingredients in it, in you know what I mean? It might have 10 different things in it. That's not pure MDMA. Molly is pure MDMA. There are different kinds of ecstasy out there, so it depends on how it was made. Like Yellow School Bus, those are good. Or the Bart Simpson. It's like certain types of ecstasy are cut up with different shit, so different tabs make you feel different ways. It gets you in the mood, the groovy dancing mood, your heart is racing at all times, like your fist is pumping, you just can't sit still. You can like chip your teeth because your teeth are chattering like when you're cold, your eyes are like pinpoints, it's an indescribable feeling, it's like you're not controlling your own body. You know, you're being controlled, you're being controlled by this drug. But it's fun, you know what I mean? All you want to do is dance, you need a lot of music, and if you drink orange juice, you know that keeps your roll going up.

Now with Molly, you don't feel the side effects, like you do when you wake up in the morning with ecstasy. Molly is so pure that it's like, you know, you have to eat more of Molly than you do ecstasy. The most I've ever eaten of E-pills was 4½ in a night and that was really bad, I was like tripping balls. That was fucking unbelievable, and that was my first rave in freshman year, summer, when I was selling the stuff.

When I've eaten Molly, I've taken only six or seven because Mollies are so pure that after two or three hours of dancing and sweating it out, the effect is going to go away. Remember, you're drinking plenty of water, you're drinking more water than you ever have before when you're on this stuff to keep yourself rolling and keep yourself hydrated, and usually this is happening at summertime, in the middle of these packed crowds, and it's so hot. Like I said, with Molly the side effects are so different, but with ecstasy you can wake up from that shit and then smoke a blunt and later on that day that shit kicks right back in because you've got heroine and ecstasy, or you've got crystal meth and ecstasy, because different kinds of ecstasy are cut up with different kinds of shit, but Molly is pure.

Soon after the Soho, I landed a job doing live infomercials, and this was for Mr. Sticky. When I first got to Miami, I'd signed up with Explore Talent, which is my talent agency, and I get a call, like, "Man, we want you for this talent opportunity so come on in for an audition!" I wound up going to the audition and I killed it. I loved it and I was like happy! I got picked out of 600 people. I was like real pumped up about it. The next thing I know, I was doing live infomercials selling the Mr. Sticky product, "The world's first lifetime guaranteed lint roller that never has the need for refills as long as you own it." I also sold the Chef's Envy slicer and the Chef's Rival chopper, which are cooking tools. One is for vegetables, the other one is for your meat. And you can put them in different compartments, and chop them all up without anything being touched together or anything. And it's real quick, without a knife. So that was cool, selling those things. I was traveling all around Miami, I mean, I was driving all the way up to West Palm Beach, I was driving down to Coral Gables, I was driving out to Kendall to give these live presentations, and I got to see everything, so it was awesome.

I'm doing my Mr. Sticky pitch in this store, doing my live infomercial for a couple of places, and this kid, Adam, I see him all the time at that location, and he's like, "You know, dude, my friend Michelle wants to talk to you." "Oh, yeah?" So I wind up talking to this girl, Michelle, and we hang out that weekend. I told Anna, Beth's friend, that I was going…oh, I forget where, but I told her I was going someplace, and I drive all the way up to Boca Raton to get with this girl Michelle…only to find out she's a recovering junkie. You know what I mean? I picked her up from a fucking sober house, we went to the movies, and I fucked her in the car Beth's parents had given us. It was like whatever. I still talk to her to this day. She's a very cool, down to earth girl, and she's still clean. I drove back to Miami, slept withBeth, whatever. You know what I mean? Like who cares, dude?

About this time I was also working at Art Basel. Art Basel is the biggest artistic event ever in Miami. About 70,000 people fly in every December for this show. It's a huge event for the arts, and all the people who love art pack into the city. It was cool to be a part of all these events, and these experiences set up my whole fashion sense, and expanded my understanding of the arts. I was also involved with organizing a number of events, which was the focus of my studies. Along with the fast-track lifestyle scene I had witnessed while working at the Soho, I began to integrate the European influence into my own personal expression.

My birthday was coming along; I'm a Capricorn, born the day before Christmas, remember? Beth wound up getting a snake for my birthday! I always wanted a snake, so she got me this snake that I named Slicktoria. She was a boa python and we got her from an 11-year old breeder. We went to see this kid at his parent's apartment in Wellington, Florida, which is two hours from Miami. I was pissed because Beth wouldn't tell me where we were going. We finally got there and this kid has about 50 different reptiles in the apartment. It was crazy! He showed me how to do the feeding and all that good stuff. When I first got her, she was very tiny, she was just a small snake. The first time I ever fed Slicktoria, Beth wasn't with me, but I had those other two girls over, my girls Jill and Chelsea, the two girls from Massachusetts. In about six months, Slicktoria had grown to over five feet long. I had to give her up when I moved out during the summer. I sold her to these two dudes who were going to use her in a porno. I didn't want to say goodbye to her, but Providence was no place for a python.

Chapter 18

Providence

I was taking trips back and forth to Providence every other month while I was in Miami, just to visit my friends.

Going back to Prov was kind of weird. Not being there, me not being around, brought our crew closer together because, remember, at the end of our sophomore year we were kind of all just verging away from each other. Without me there, and once the Washington house ended, everybody split up. I moved to Miami, Cheese was cheap and never had an apartment though he was always hanging out at other crew members' apartments, Trups moved to Denver to go to school after he stole from me, and P-Money and Muggs wound up getting an apartment together at University Heights. Turbs and Milla, they dropped out of school. Turbs dropped out at the end of junior year and Milla dropped out at the start of senior year. So it was weird going back, everything not being the same, and like the game had changed, you know what I mean? We didn't have all the crazy resources we once had.

One time I got a call from my crew that P-Money got pulled over on Thayer Street up near Brown University by a Massachusetts narcotics agent. One of our buddies named Riley, who wound up being a snake in the grass, had gotten into some beef with a kid and he'd stabbed this kid. Riley is a 6 foot 5" white kid with scruffy hair, and he'd fucking stabbed this kid. For some reason, Riley said he lived out at P-Money's house, the old house on Washington Street, so the Feds were like following us, you know, they knew us from the year before, from all the drugs and shit we had, so now they pulled P-Money over and they're searching everybody, and this happened once when I was actually there.

So I'm there visiting, and we all go out to eat, and I'm in the car with Muggs and we're pulled over by these cops, and the detectives are pulling us out, yanking us out. "Which one of you is Riley? Where are the knives? Where are all the drugs? Where's the house? Where's everything? Who's the connect?" and I'm like, "What the fuck are you talking about? I'm up here visiting my boys, I live in Miami, I don't live here anymore!" "Don't lie to me! Who lived on Washington Street? ..." and I'm like, "Dude, nobody lives there anymore!" Like that is so old, you know what I mean? "Hey! None of those kids are even here anymore!" So they let us go, but we still felt kind of hot, like we were under surveillance and shit, you know what I mean? It was kind of weird, but we wound up beating through all of that. Lame brains.

So like I said, I was visiting Prov every two months or so, and every single time I went back, I got into a fight with those same kids from PSP. They saw me and just wanted to tear me up because of what happened with that Asian kid at the end of the summer and how I shamed their whole fraternity. The last time we'd fought was on my January trip.

I'm hanging out in Prov, and my buddy Buck, the guy from Hawaii who was in the Marines, was hanging out with me. Cheese is with us, too. We go to this house, and we pull up, and we have the whole crew. We've got the two Infinitys packed out, plus the Jeep Wrangler, and we're going in there with the goon squad.

There are 30 of these PSP kids and just eight or nine of us. We get there, we rollout, and we have Serge, and we also have a giant dude named Brown, and these are the two bodyguards of our group, you know, big as hell, and we also have P-Money, Milla, Turbs, everybody's there, so we just pretty much get into a huge brawl with these kids, I mean we fuck these kids up. I get out of the car, and just punch this one kid in the face. This kid is hurt bad. You know, just knocked him out. He gets up, and yells, "King Kong ain't got shit on me!" and Serge picked him up by the neck and literally threw this kid over the gate. The kid woke up later on...

This was how that went, and it all started because of Cheese. They were insulting Cheese, and he's my boy, and we're always going to look out for him. It was their way of getting to me because the real reason for the shit was they all wanted to fight me. They knew that if they could get at Cheese, they were going to find me. I'm going to come out of the woodwork, you know?

We actually wound up meeting them again later on that night, after clubbing. And that was our last fight. We ran into each other on the street and we had this massive brawl. Serge just clothes-lined these kids, you know, and we just started fighting from there. I mean everybody was pulling out knives, a kid got thrown up onto a dumpster, it was crazy shit.

I went back again in March for St. Patty's Day. I'd been back there five times since the summer and I fought every time, you know, over that same stupid beef, so this time I show up in Prov and they don't want to fight. They wanted to squash everything, so we all shook hands and everybody was cool. But we get to the bar and Serge is like, "You know what, Vic? Fuck these kids! Don't accept their apology." Serge was walking around me and he's got on this security shirt, and I mean, he's like, "Do whatever you want, Vic." Serge liked being our muscle, and he was aching for more action, so I'm throwing beers in these kids' faces and slapping the beers out of their hands…I'm doing whatever I want while getting hammered. I'm getting belligerently shit-faced at this bar, with Serge backing me up. Even so, I get kicked out of the bar, you know what I mean? In the morning I wake up on Milla's couch.

One of my favorite places is Mount Fuji. I'm hanging out at Milla's and I'm about to leave the next day. It's my last two days in Prov and I want to get a nice little lunch and dinner, sit with everybody, hang out, have some drinks. I take everybody out to this new place across the street that's called Mount Fuji.

It's a nice little steakhouse on Dean Street. Lots of nice neon lighting, real sexy feel, good sushi, a great menu, and an awesome presentation. They're just opening up, and I wind up being very well-known there. I'm like taking pictures with the owner and my picture's on the wall with the owner, you know? I've been there since the first day they opened and there's a lot of love shown, and all the bartenders, especially Sam and Diana, they love me, you know what I mean? I had my own drink menu there, and later on when I returned to Providence for my senior year, my parents were with me, and the owners came out to eat with us, and everything was comped, the meals, the drinks, you know what I mean? And they gave my parents my drink menu, and my food menu, and it was just an awesome good time.

Chapter 19

I Get Robbed ... and Lose My Girl

After that I headed back to Miami. And even though I haven't been running drugs seriously since before the summer, I still have a lot of cash stashed in my apartment. Honestly, I probably had about $10,000. Cash. It was stashed in shoe boxes. And I got robbed.

My fucking barber came through my apartment with a bunch of goons. They ran in there with like guns and shit. AK-47s, and all this extra terrestrial shit, and literally stuck us up. Me and my buddies are in there and we're about to go to the beach and shit, you know? We're just hanging out, smoking blunt, chilling, and all of a sudden these goons come crashing through the door, and I got tazed, I got tazered full blast. Fuck!

Another kid got pistol-whipped, and these goons were running around the apartment, checking through all the rooms, robbing the entire house. They got a lot of stuff, but they also missed a lot, though they got a lot of the stuff they came for. They wound up shooting the gun off, and the cops came. So now the cops are running around the house and this turns into a big, big thing, but I never told my parents because I'm old enough and now it's all on me. One of the kids with me heard this guy's name, and so that dude got arrested. I don't want to give this guy's name up; I'm not that kind of guy, so whatever. But this story went on for a long time because they wanted me to go testify and this and that, and I was very nervous. I didn't want to fuck around with this, you know? And by then I'd already moved back to Providence for my senior year. It was terrible. It was all happening at the wrong time. I wasn't financially stable enough to see this through. I didn't want to get my parents involved, but I also didn't have the right amount of money to help or anything like that. So I just left it where it was. I left it alone. I never testified. Nobody else did. You know, we left it at that. The dude probably got away; I don't know anything else about it. But that was a bad trip. Real bad. AK-47s, man. Fucking tazers?

Shit. Now me and Beth are starting to break up. I felt things going off the deep end. Me and her mom had multiple arguments after that first time, and her mom wanted her to come home. They were trying to get her away from me. They had pretty much made a deal with her, "Oh, Honey, we want you to go back to the Providence campus…and tell Vic to go fuck himself." So Beth told me she had to go back to Providence because she needed a certain college credit, or there was a class she had to take and she had to transfer, or something dumb that didn't make sense. So I'm flipping out. I'm like, "Yeah, we came out here as a couple, right? I'm taking care of you, and now you're just going to up and leave? She's like, "No, I want you to come, too."

Now we're looking into transferring and I wind up talking to my ex-girlfriend, Lynia, again 'cause I was asking her, "Damn, what the hell do you think this girl is doing? And what should I do? Do I leave her? Do I not?" You know? And Lynia said to just play along with it. So I played along with it. I wound up getting my transfer papers, and then boom! I'm ready to head back to Providence for my senior year.

The school year is almost over and now Beth is getting even more weird. At the end of every year, the Miami campus has a Bash at the Beach event. Everybody from the school goes to the beach and has a good time, kind of like a party for all the kids to say goodbye and jump into summer. Beth and her friends wanted to go, but McKenzie didn't want me to go because she knew every girl at that campus wanted to talk to me. I was the fresh face and had been fly all year! Of course, I wanted to go for the same reason Beth didn't want me to go, because it was going to be awesome, man, but okay. You don't want me to go? I won't go. So we made a deal that neither of us would go. Beth and her friends said they'd go somewhere else that day, and that's what I told them I'd do, too. So we both promised not to go, but I go anyway. I took one of my girls with me and we're having a good time, you know? Food, surf, sun, fun…and then Josh taps me on the shoulder. "Vic, Beth's right behind you!" I turn around and there she is, Beth and her droids. They popped up anyway, just like I did. So nowBeth's pissed at me because I went to this event when I said I wouldn't, and I'm with this cute girl, Karina, on the beach, which was Beth's biggest fear, and it just became this big ugly thing.

We got through that somehow, and it's time. Beth's all ready to move back to Providence but I still have to take a summer class, so I'm going to be staying in Miami for most of the summer. Beth's stuff is packed and shipped, and we get our last kiss at the airport. And she's gone.

I went home to Pennsylvania for a few days before my summer class started, and then, since I'm home, I went to my second rave ever, with all my buddies.

Now I just got dumped, or am on the verge of getting dumped. My buddy, Hanesworth, who was the first kid I ever did coke with, well, his girlfriend has just left him. Hanesworth's dad is CEO of ShopRite, and Hanesworth took care of this girl all four years of college, and after they graduated, on the day of their graduation, she left him. And we're with my buddy Sabby, and he moved to New York with his girl after he graduated, when I moved to Miami with my girl, and now he just got dumped, and we're all getting fucking dumped! It's like Venus is in retrograde or some such shit, you know? So this was all very weird. Anyway, we're at this rave, and I'm hanging out with Janeway, I'm hanging out with Cheese, I'm hanging out with Steve Platinum. You know, we're just raving it up, we have our whole rave crew, there are about 40 of us, a bunch of girls and shit, and we all had a great time!

I get back to Miami and my buddy, Jason Lewis, came down to Miami with me. We hung out in the bars, we went to the beach, we did everything, and we wound up going to Fort Lauderdale. We're hanging out, having a good time, you know?

Lo and behold, the next day Beth's dad called me. "I need you to stay away from Beth, Vic. Leave her alone, don't look her up, just stay away. We're trying to get her to stop talking to you, so don't bother her anymore, hear me?" I'm like, "What, dude? Let her make that decision," you know? But, no, he starts talking about the robbery and shit, like, "What the fuck are you doing to my daughter?" And I said like, "Hey, bro, I didn't have any drugs in the house. I only had cash, man. Like, you know it's my house. I had cash in there. You know?" Well, he's like, "Beth could've been in danger!" I'm like, "Dude, Beth wasn't even around. They wouldn't have hurt Beth. That's one thing they wouldn't have done, they don't harm girls." You know? But he didn't want to hear it, so whatever.

Anyway, now Beth was really acting weird. I'm trying to hit her up, and she's acting like she didn't even know any of this shit was going on. I'm like, wow, what the fuck is this? So then I started sensing it, you know? She finally hit me up, and she was acting funny. She said, "You know, Vic, I really can't talk to you anymore. Like my parents said if I talk to you, they're going to kick me out and I'd have to go back to Miami, and I need some time to think, Vic," and she started to cry and shit… So now I'm starting to break down, too, and I'm starting to cry because I'm like, well, damn, she left me while I was in this position. It was cold, you know?

I was upset about the breakup, but I was even more upset about the position she left me in with this whole robbery situation going on. I don't know what the fuck she told her parents, and they were getting involved in shit they didn't need to be involved in. You know? They were calling me, threatening me with all kinds of shit, and I'm like, dude, I'll fucking buy you motherfuckers, like fuck you! So they're all pissed off, whatever. I went through this crazy stage; I didn't eat for a week or two, and I barely scarfed down a meal. I would go to my summer class every day, and when I got out, I would literally work out the rest of the day. I'd smoke packs of cigarettes every day, drink wine, and just work out. You know, to cope with this loss and the way Beth totally vaporized.

Funny thing is, I went from fucking all those women in Providence to fucking just a few in Miami. But at the end of the day, I'm not going to bash this girl, you know what I mean? I still love her, like she's a great girl. I know Beth is going to read this, and I have nothing bad to say about her. She's a great girl, she did everything. It was me, because I was a fucked up individual. I wasn't a person who was ready to settle down.

It's true, though. There was a point where I felt like getting married and having kids. I did that shit when I was 20-21 years old, you know? I lived with my girl, and I know how that shit goes, I know the lifestyle, I know what it's like to make breakfasts, make the bed, do the laundry, pay the bills, and dream the dream of life together forever. Just all that kind of stuff. And me and Beth had a lot of great times, and we had a lot of bad times. A lot of the bad times was her going through my phone and finding me cheating, texting other girls, and this and that. You know, just different things like that and stuff. But aside from that, our time was perfect. I'm not ready to settle down just yet. I'd rather have 10 wives than one, you know?

Anna, the Spanish Anna, she was definitely a big help when Beth left me and shit. Anna picked me up at the airport when I got back to Miami, and she hung out with me while I was finishing that summer class, but then she left for the summer, so I really had nobody there with me. I was just alone. Everybody was gone. Drew was gone because he and my fuck buddy Stacy had left in spring trimester to go back to Providence. My bro Josh had gone back to Georgia for the summer, Anna went home to the Dominican, Beth had dumped me, Emily had taken off for the summer…so I'm out there for the next six weeks, fucking pulling my hair out and shit, you know, but…

But I got through it. It was nothing. You know, I got through it.

I was talking to my buddy, Bobo the junkie, and he was like, "Yo, dude, come on up for the summer, man. Come to Boston! It'll be no problem. We'll move into an apartment and you can work with me and my family for the summer where we'll have mass fun! We'll have a good time, man!" So I said, "Yeah, dude, that's awesome," so when my summer class was over, I was eager to go. My parents came down the last two weeks I was there, helped me get my stuff packed, you know, just take me out and shit, see how I was doing, and then my buddy P-Money and his two cousins came down and we had a blast. We went to a bunch of bars, partied, brought a bunch of chicks back to the apartment, and helped me pack up my stuff. Then we had this yacht party. We were on this yacht in the Keys, and it was an awesome time. This was my last week in Miami, and I left in good style.

Just before I left, I met Dennis Rodman. Rodman tried to pick us up at this bar. He was, "Yeah, when you five guys from Brooklyn are ready to get into the industry, and you have to start banging dudes, give me a call." And like we're just shocked, like what the fuck? I'm talking to Rodman, and he's a cool cat. I just want to learn about him, you know? Well, my buddies are like, "No way, dude, fuck him! He's a homo, stay away!" I said, "Wait a minute, the man's a fucking billionaire almost." So I'm kicking it with Rodman, and it was an overall good time.

I said my goodbyes to Miami, and as soon as I got back to Providence, Muggs and Bobo picked me up at the airport.

Chapter 20

Back in Prov

They have bottles, and weed, and Bobo just got out of rehab, so he's not supposed to be drinking or anything, and I'm going to be a sponsor for him for the rest of the summer, and whatever. We wind up getting hammered, and then Muggs leaves to go on a cruise. Me and Bobo drive back to his place, and when we get there, Bobo has this girl waiting for me, like this chick who goes to Harvard, a real smart girl. We're having a little party, and then Bobo goes upstairs to sleep and leaves me down there with his girl, and we're talking. Of course I wind up fucking her, you know. She studied in Cambridge and she was pretty smart, so like Lil' Wayne sings, "She give me good brain like she studied at Cambridge", ha ha! It was cool, that was definitely perfect! It was a great way to come home to Prov.

I worked the rest the summer with Bobo, I mean we did massive events. His family had a slushie company called Dave and Jerry's Italian Ice that grossed over $1.5 million every summer, it's like a five-month thing from May to late September, and we did about 150 - 200 events. Yeah, it was an awesome time, and it was happening all the way into the fall.

We got our apartments, and I got this dope apartment downtown, a massive loft right above the biggest lake in Providence, smack-dab downtown prime location, you know, and I'm bringing chicks over, and we're taking trips back and forth to the Foxwoods Resort Casino in Connecticut. I'm hanging out with his girl, Alyssa Migs; we called her Smiggs, so it's like me, Bobo, Smiggs, and these other girl Sheridan and Sullivan.

Then Milla came back. Milla and Bobo were planning to live together for the year. Of course, Bobo just got out of rehab, so Milla's not supposed to bring any drugs around, but Milla brings in three ounces of cocaine and leaves it with me at the house with Bobo. And he's like, "Yo, dude, don't let Bobo touch it, you know what I mean? Unless he has money." So as soon as Milla leaves, Bobo gives me all the money he earned that day, and he says, "Here, bro, let's get an 8-ball. Let's start blowing coke before we go out tonight!"

So we start blowing lines, and I'm like, whatever! And I'm like, "Dude, you're not supposed to be blowing shit, you know!" So I told Bobo, "Listen, dude, we're both grownups, we're both the same age. I'll be your sponsor but if you're going to make dumb decisions with your shit, that's on you, bro. You know? I told you once not do this shit, but you know what? I'm going to do this shit with you, and that's it, we're going to do this together, and if you're doing it without me, then you have a problem." So we started blowing coke and we wound up blowing two 8-balls that night. And Bobo wound up junking out again.

That summer we got a bunch of chicks from a bar underneath Milla's place called Nara's, and we started acting out with these girls. We were taking them to random hotels, spending dumb money, fucking these chicks day and night, you know? Just whatever, having a good summer. We had Foxwoods, we had drugs, we had bars, we had girls...it was a great summer. I even slept with Smiggs, but I didn't actually get to fuck her since we wound up passing out together.

Chowder was there, his girl Andrea was there, there was a bunch of stuff going on, and then I met this new girl, Arielle P. She's the same age as me, same year as me, same class as me. She's one of the Phi Sig sisters, and I just never met her. I'm like, where the hell were you? You know? I make it my business to meet everybody but I never met her! So now she and I are hanging out, and she's like, "Yeah, you know, Vic, I have something special to tell you. When a guy comes in my mouth, I'll bust all over the bed!" I'm like, "Get the fuck out of here! You're a squirter? Wow, you're a squirter! I'm down!" So I get a couple of bags of coke from Milla, take this girl to my apartment and Arielle gave me head. As soon as I came in her mouth, she literally squirted all over my bed! It was like unreal! I'm fucking this girl like all night, you know, and it was like the craziest fuck, and I wound up really falling for this chick, like damn, like this chick is everything I need! You know, like she's the full package!

It was a great way to set me up for my senior year. It was like getting back on the grind, getting back on the roll, and I started getting back into selling a little bit.

Muggs returned from the cruise, you know, we're hanging out doing all types of crazy shit again, and like I said, we've got the cocaine back. We didn't have as much as we did in our sophomore year, we only had a couple of ounces, you know, just to sell, make a couple of dollars, but we're cool, we're just rolling with it. We blew coke from July to November. We blew coke every single day. That was crazy, that was just like sick. It was really sickening, and it was all good.

Senior Year

Chapter 21

Stroking It

The summer ended pretty much with me, Bobo, Milla, and the girls hanging out. We had these two girls from Nara's, Victoria and Sarah. We hung out with them a lot, and we did a lot of drugs with them. They were a cool pair of chicks, lots of laughter, lots of fun, and good in bed, too. Just the thing for those lazy summer afternoons, you know? The air was slightly cool in the apartment with the air conditioning on, and our noses were full of powder…then me and Victoria would feel the rush and run into the bedroom, strip off whatever clothing we had left, and just stroke the time away…I really like afternoon fucking because I know all the poor Joes are out there in their daily jobs, minding the boss while I'm inside a hot chick on a hot day. There's nothing like it! It didn't matter if it was Victoria or Sarah…they were both sweet in the sack, and they loved to fuck me.

Now the last school year was about to start. And we were throwing this huge event, the first party of the year. It was for the new freshmen and it was at Club

Ultra with Cheese spinning the discs. Club Ultra is over on Pine Street, and there are some nice looking ladies that show up there all the time! Long legs in short skirts and mesh nylons...and all kinds of booty. Boobs and booty on these stylin' babes. Yeah, yeah, yeah, there are some real dogs, too...but there's also some great pussy. I know you know what I mean.

So we're throwing this welcome party for the new freshmen, and the way we connected was by helping them move into the dorms. Cheese and me are moving boxes, meeting these kids, and inviting them to our party, which was going to be the next day. We wanted all of them to come, and this was a great way to meet them. Meet the dudes, sure, but also meet the new ladies... It's the first party of the year, and that's what you do, you have a party to welcome the freshmen and show them a good time. We were also helping the sorority girls rush kids, too, you know. The freshmen don't know what the hell was going on, so this is a chance to meet them and show them the ropes...and by helping our sorority girls, we knew we would probably also find lots of new ass. Think about it... These girls are looking to get laid, too. Remember, they're just escaping their Mommy/Daddy prisons and looking for crazy!

So the day before the party we were moving all these new kids into the dorms. I remember that was the first day I had seen Beth since our breakup in the early part of summer, about two months before.

Yeah, that was kind of a weird moment. Did that ever happen to you? You see a girl or dude you've been so into for so long, and now you know there's nothing there anymore? Whatever you had is gone, like forever, and even the memories of what you had are starting to blink and fade out. It's a weird moment when you see that person, especially when you're not expecting it. It's kind of like a shock.

When I saw her in front of Gaebe Commons, I wanted Beth to know she didn't matter to me anymore, and I also wanted her to know what she was missing. Besides, I'd been laid by over a dozen women since I'd seen her at the Miami airport when we said goodbye, so I picked up this other girl, Steph, one of my sorority sisters with giant tits who was standing next to me, and I started kissing her, just fucking around, you know, and I could see Beth's face, and she was just like in awe. Her face was saying, "I can't believe you just did that!" And that was about it for me and Beth in senior year...

A few weeks later we had this huge party called The Launch. Me, Milla, Michael Cohen, Cheese, Christopher Reeve, and Jay Healy put our money together and threw this event at the ice skating rink. It was a block from my apartment, downtown on Washington Street. I was all xannied out, I was on Maui, I was on Coke, I was on everything that night.

When I got back to my apartment, I called Beth up, and had a conversation with her. I wanted to clear things up, put things on the table. I didn't want her anymore, you know. Once we were done for the summer, I was over her. I really don't remember much about the call because of the Xanax, so it's all pretty vague, but we had this big, big, BIG argument that went on for a long time, and that was a mess, and then, after the argument, I hit her up the next day. She's like, let's go get some lunch or something, and so I said I was totally down. But then we wound up not doing lunch, or anything; we were just being nice, I guess. I only saw her twice in senior year. The first time was when I was moving the kids into the dorm and I grabbed and kissed Steph, and then two weeks after that somewhere on campus. I never saw Beth ever again after that.

And you know, my heart wasn't hurting. Not at all. When I got back to Prov after summer, like I said, the first thing that happened was I got laid in my first 24 hours in town by that brainy chick from Harvard. I was on a roll. I was doing my thing. I had about 10 girls that summer and then in fall trimester I was hitting girls left and right. I had so many girls, it was unbelievable. I was back on my grind. All I needed to do was be in Providence and I was back on top. Literally!

So anyway, Cheese and I moved these new kids into the dorms, and I was helping my sisters rush for the sorority while promoting this cool party.

It was the night of our party and we're getting ready to go out, and Cheese is spinning the event. We wound up buying a bunch of decorations and floor prizes and stuff like that, but my buddy, Devin, came in and threw a rival move. He had a party at the club on the ground floor of my apartment building, which was Club Roxy. It's a bigger club and he literally stole all the freshmen from us! Most of them went to the Roxy, and we barely broke even. A lot of people left our event to pack the Roxy, but I couldn't leave Cheese sitting there. He DJ'd the event, so our kids had a good time, but it wasn't as huge as we'd planned it to be. I had a good time 'powdering my nose', you know, and working the new freshmen girls.

Senior year was a lot of partying, and a lot of going out. As the new school year started rolling along, we had a bunch of coke flowing through our hands again; not as much as before, but we had enough, and we're all getting hammered to go out for the night, every night, and we're taking out the freshmen girls who are thrilled to be connecting with us bad-ass seniors.

I called them "my bitches". That was Carley, Elyse, Priscilla, Chloe, and Heather. We picked these girls up to go to the club. I had Muggs's Infinity, and we're ready to pregame; we head back to my place to get drunk, and then we're going out for the night. We're all trying to drive Muggs's Infinity, and everyone is arguing. We eventually got over to the Pembroke houses, the houses over by the college, and we're about to go into this party there, but the next thing we know, we've all split up.

We met up with some of our other crew members like P-Money, Serge, all of these guys, and we're all walking down Pembroke Avenue. We're all 22 years old and have red cups in our hands, and the cops stop us and want to check our IDs, which was the funniest shit in the world! But Milla had coke on him, so Milla fled. He just started flat-out running. This woman cop tried to grab him but Milla elbowed her right above her lip; she grabbed onto his shirt and Milla slipped out of it and ran. The next thing we heard were two shots fired down the street! Blam! Blam! The police fired their weapons two or three times. It was scary! They were shooting at Milla, trying to get him to stop. And remember, it's packed out. Every street is packed! It's the beginning of the new school year, and everybody is out partying. So it's crazy!

We didn't know if Milla was hurt or dead or what. The cops were chasing him. We went to the sorority house and looked in the attic, and sure enough, there's Milla. He's like, "Shit! I need some new clothes!"

The cops had every street shut down. We whipped around in P-Money's Infinity, the silver one with no tints or anything. P-Money had a suit and tie on so he looked like he was just a business guy on his way out of town or something. It was like four in the morning when this was happening. P-Money picked up Milla, we threw him in the trunk, and he and P-Money made it through the police line.

Chapter 22

Xanax Rules

Next week, Milla comes back and now some other shit happens. We're over by the Pembroke houses, Muggs is coked out, drunk as hell, and winds up crashing his Infinity! He's hammered, and I don't even know why he was driving. We're all on drugs, and we all got mixed up that night. I was at some other party doing some crazy shit, and now Muggs gets a DUI and loses his license. So that sucked.

This was when Milla left Providence for good. He dropped out of college, early in senior year. Milla came to my apartment one morning at 7:00 a.m., all coked out, and dropped off about two ounces of coke. And a pack of cigarettes. And he said, "Guy, just hold this down for me," and then he left.

So I go to Muggs later and I say, "Yo! Like Milla just dropped off some mad coke. What do we do with this shit?" You know? Muggs is like, "Well, clearly, we're going to just do it all." So me and Muggs blew lines every day, and I don't even know for how many months.

But here's the other part of that story.

Before Milla left, he started robbing from me and Muggs. He was taking mad shit from us. Shit was just going missing, and when he was there, the stuff showed up again. It didn't take long to figure out he was ripping us.

Milla had no apartment because Bobo had junked out and had to go home and get back into rehab. Bobo started doing so much coke he was never sober, and he also started getting into the blues and shooting up heroin. Bobo was right back in it, hard and heavy, shooting up at the end of the summer and the start of the school year, so Milla had to move out of the apartment with Bobo or go down with him. Milla tried to move in with me and Muggs, and we told him, "No, you can't live here, dude. You know? Your trip is too dope ass for us," and then Milla started stealing from us. Little bits of cash went missing; and we'd just got the i-Phone 5 so some accessories disappeared; little shit like our bowls and bongs were gone...it was all very weird. He stole everything he could get his hands on. He was just junking out, and this kid became a serious fiend.

Everybody had the code to my door, and my apartment was literally like a fucking public bathroom. I would come home from class and there would be random people in my crib, you know what I mean? Like nobody would ever steal, but with Milla, one day we caught his ass stealing. So it was fucked up. When we caught him, he didn't say anything. And that's when he showed up the next morning at 7:00 a.m., gave me a bunch of coke and a pack of cigs, said he was sorry and asked me to stash the coke for him. That was the last time we saw Milla.

In my apartment building there was this kid named Biscuit, another kid named Garrett, and also my cousin Chuck. We used to have huge parties there, and one time we had a blowout party called a Vicapalooza, named after me. It was a riot!

Biscuit was this tall, heavier white kid. We called him Biscuit because he was soft and white like a biscuit. And this kid was like such a little bitch. You know? So we called him Biscuit.

Because we each had our own apartments in this building, when we had parties we'd open up all four doors so our guests could wander from apartment to apartment. We'd blow a horn and then everybody had to go to the next apartment, and each apartment had its own theme and a different set of drinks. It was cool, you know?

Of course there were a couple of fights. The first fight was between Chuck and Biscuit. They lived in the building before I got there, and then when I got there, everything changed. Chuck and I were close, so that put off Biscuit, and that led to the apartment wars.

Biscuit was fucking around with my cousin, and Chuck is fucking around with my boy Biscuit's door. So we're fucking up Biscuit's door, spraying shaving cream and doing all kinds of shit like that. Then we egg his apartment. We also egg Chuck's apartment and even go outside and egg his windows. Now Chuck has raw egg dripping all around his crib. After that we put syrup all over his door handle. And then rubbed garlic on it! So now he's mad, really mad.

And we were with these girls. There was Courtney, Teria, and this other chick who looked like Dennis Rodman. We gave them some gooey stuff to mix up, a bunch of crap like fish, onions, hot sauce and everything, and we were going to have them knock on Chuck's door and throw it in his face. So all this crazy shit was going on with these apartment wars. I left Biscuit's apartment to go upstairs for a moment and when I came back down, Chuck was super mad and had his fist up in front of Biscuit's face, and he's threatening to punch Biscuit in the nose. Chuck's yelling at him to come outside, literally screaming, "I want to punch you in your fucking face!" Of course, Biscuit doesn't want to come out, but then these two started going at it right there in the hallway. It was pretty funny, you know? Crazy, but funny.

Garrett was the kid who lived next door to Biscuit. He was my boy since freshman year. Garrett was like a computer techie nerd dude. And he was the reason why me and Muggs got back into the Xanax game, because Garrett was like the kid in the movie 'Charlie Bartlett'. Garrett actually said exactly what Charlie Bartlett did in the movie, just so he could get Xanax pills. The school wound up believing Garrett was crazy and had depression and all this other stuff, and they wound up giving him Xanax. Like every two weeks Garrett was getting the full prescription. So he was giving me, Muggs, and all of us bottles of Xanax. You know what I mean? Free drugs from the school! We were having an awesome time!

The thing about Xanax is it's like a blackout pill. Me and Muggs would just abuse them, you know? We'd take the pills and then drink alcohol and get drunk, and when you drink on Xanax you don't remember anything. We call them bars because they look like a little bar. "Two Xanax and I'm fantasizin', 'bout that bitch's panty sizes..." When you eat two Xanax, that's the kind of shit you're feeling. You don't know what you're doing; you have no clue until you wake up. Like I busted my nose senior year on a set of stairs because I was all xannied out, and I was drunk, and I was all fucked up at this party, and I literally cracked my fucking face on the stairs. I wound up fucking this girl, Lissa; I couldn't believe I fucked her, like this real fat chick!

Mind you, fucking a fat girl is pretty interesting stuff. I would never have thought much about it, except the usual reaction, but it can actually be a very curious experience. In fact, I recommend it! No, I know...you think I'm crazy. Only those girls who are slim and trim for you, huh? But I'm telling you, don't knock it if you haven't tried it. I'm not talking about the morbidly obese, okay? But an occasional BBW can be good for your soul. Try it and you'll see.

Anyway, we're taking this blackout drug because we're going out, and that's how me and Muggs are, five feet eight nothing, and that's what we're here to do, we're here to pop drugs, we're here to wow out, we're the life of the party, you know what I mean? We want to be blacked out, and we don't want to remember shit. I mean, really, we're two short, reckless kids. It's our senior year, and it's depressing enough knowing that school is about done, you know? The four year vacation is almost over, dude.

Besides, it was a fun drug to take. You only really blackout if you abuse it and drink on it. Like we did! We would take like four or five Xans a night and then just drink, you know what I mean? It would take four or five of them to get us hammered.

Xanax is an antidepressant. It's going to make you feel mellowed out, but it also makes you forget everything that's going on. It's like getting some relief from your problems instead of smoking a cigarette. It completely moves everything.

Viva! Viva la Mexico! Viva was this bar, and we were always hanging out there with our kids, like Mark, and Cohen, and these kids were like hosting this bar, and we were there and we killed it, man. We had an awesome fucking time at Viva. Viva was every Friday night, and me and Muggs would go there fucked up on drugs. It was just two doors down from my apartment building, like just a hop away, literally right next door, so we'd go there so fucking late. I knew the owner, so I'd just walk in, and he and I would blow coke together, and I would get free drinks and shit...it was amazing, and I was like the life of Viva.

There was also the Colosseum over on Pine Street. That was another great club. You haven't seen Providence until you've been to see the Colosseum's foam parties, the wet T-shirt contests, jello-wrestling, and the lingerie fashion shows... Marky Mac was the young kid hosting that club. He would let us in there for freebies, free drink passes, and free girls. That was my idea of a great club!

Chapter 23

Crash!

It's Halloween, my favorite worst holiday of the year. It was the night before Halloween, which was when Muggs and Rainstorm broke up. They were arguing and whatever, and Muggs leaves this party; Cheese was DJing there. Rainstorm pulls me aside and says, "Vic, I need to talk to you. Yo," she says, "tell Muggs I don't want him anymore, like tell him to leave me alone, like I am done with him, like I can't deal with him, you know. He's all fucked up on drugs and shit..." And I'm like, "Well, Rainstorm, that's fucked up. You've been doing this kid dirty, you know, like, fuck you."

Whatever. I mean, the background to this is Muggs and Rainstorm had a bumpy relationship, you know? It had hardly ever been smooth between them; they were drawn to each other by sex and love and time, but that's not always enough. And sometimes you're with the wrong person but you can't let go. So you need to hold on through the bumps and scrapes and crashes and your heart gets beaten up until you just get worn out and can't take it anymore. You just get to a place where you have to give up or die.

I mean, Muggs was getting fucked up all the time and a lot of it was overRainstorm, you know? He'd get high and drive over to Rainstorm's place, and one night he got there and saw the light on in her upstairs bedroom window, and there was a guy's shadow silhouetted on the curtain. Boom! The light went out and then when Muggs knocked on the door, Rainstorm and this dude were pretending they were downstairs the whole time. So what was up with that, you know? Rainstorm was a bit iffy sometimes, and though she was never caught with a dude, something was up; we didn't know what. Even if she was faithful, the relationship wasn't right for either of them and it had to end. It was driving them both nuts.

So I spoke to Muggs, "Muggs, like Rainstorm is pretty much done, bro, you know what I mean? Like let this bitch rock out. You know what I'm saying?" Muggs was pretty well tired of her, too, so he got it.

What happened next was Rainstorm called me on Halloween morning, while Muggs was crashed out, and she said to me, "Yo, I have to meet up with you. I have to give you the kid's shit back," so I'm like okay, whatever, so she came down to my apartment, and we sat in front of my apartment, and we went out and ate breakfast and shit, and she's like, "Yo, I don't want to be with Muggs anymore," and like talking all this shit, and I kind of felt bad, because here I am, hanging out with Rainstorm, you know what I mean? But she called me a friend, and me and Rainstorm were friends first, since before I even knew Muggs. So I told Muggs, "Listen, bro, talk to this bitch, you know? She's a whore, bro, and leave her alone. Like leave her be." And so he left her alone. They had finally crashed and burned.

Me and Muggs went out that night for Halloween. We hung out with my sorority twin, Angie Show. She's this unfuckingbelievable dope chick, and she literally looks like a Kardashian. She has double B tits, she's from New York, and she's just absolutely beautiful. A young goddess! Angie has a boyfriend and they're tight, lucky dog. Man, but she's dope! We hung out with her and did a bunch of cocaine, got hammered and enjoyed flying through the night with her. We went to Finnegans but got kicked out. There was no fight or anything; it was just a bad night so I was acting a little crazy and got carried away. I was feeling bad for Muggs, so I guess I was being a bit more rude than usual. So that was how Halloween went down that year.

Oh, yeah. The other crash was Muggs's car. The night before Halloween, just before Muggs and Rainstorm broke it off, we all went out on the town. We pregamed at my place with the hot freshman girls, Carly, Elyse, Chloe and Priscilla. We were whipping the Infinity that night, me, Cheese, Chuck, Milla and Muggs. That's when Muggs and Rainstorm began arguing, so Muggs decided he was going to drive home hammered, and he had a bunch of coke in the car. Somehow we all got split up and Muggs and Milla were the only two still left with the car. As Muggs was pulling out of the parking space, BOOM! ...he crashed the car and one of his tires fucking popped off! And the airbags exploded! It was crazy. Muggs and Milla were both fucked up, and Milla jumped out of the car and ran off leaving the coke and old drunk Muggs sitting there in his fucking car! The next day we're trying to figure out what's going on, and that's when Rainstorm asked me to go out for breakfast and then told me she wanted no part of Muggs.

But when they broke up, that's when me and Muggs got real close. Me and Muggs were totally cool, and we got real tight. We chilled every day...every single fucking day. From then on out. Me and Muggs, chilling. I'd get out of class, and we'd go smoke weed up at his apartment. We lived on the same street; he lived at the Regency Plaza and I lived at the Washington Avenue apartments. It was kind of dope, you know what I mean? We both lived right smack downtown, had dope ass apartments, and we're hitting up a lot of chicks.

Cheese's girlfriend was Lexington. She had these three girls she hung out with, Heather, Princess, and Olivia. I used to hook up with Princess, but I actually did fuck Olivia. So that was kind of weird. And Muggs, he fucked Heather, and so we were hanging out with them. It was stuff like that going on.

And Cheese was kind of playing around with bitches. We'd never seen Cheese playing around with any girls, you know? I was also fucking this freshman named Courtney, this skinny blonde chick. She was like a 'hood ass bitch from Jersey. She was cute, you know, and she was like my main fuck for a few weeks. But then she got kicked out of school because she got caught with too much weed in her room. She was one of the best fucks I've ever had, especially being younger than me, you know? She had blonde hair, blue eyes, and skinny thighs and could open her mouth really wide! I didn't really get to see her all that much because she was gone so fast, and she didn't get to enjoy her freshman year much, either. So I began fucking her roommate, Megan. I was just catching up after all that lost time with you-know-who and trying to hit the 100-bodies' mark. Damn! I didn't hit it. I wound up reaching only 99.

Thanksgiving...time to go home. I drove Muggs's Infinity to Pennsylvania for the long weekend. Muggs was the passenger since he couldn't drive. I drove Muggs to his parents' home and left him and the car there; my parents drove over to pick me up and take me home for the holiday. It was all just weird, and getting weirder.

Chapter 24

Little Miss Ugly

Every January the Phi Sigma Sigma sorority hosts a Little Miss Ugly Pageant to support the March of Dimes. Dudes take the roles of chicks and dress up in women's clothing, wigs, makeup...so it's like a drag show, very funny, and it raises money for a good cause. It's performed at the big JWU auditorium...big stage, massive seating, you get the idea. It's a big deal.

Cheese was supposed to perform, but then he didn't want to and chickened out, so I joined at the last minute. Because it was an event being held by Beth's sorority, many of whom were my girls, I was all for it. The sorority girls said, "We need you to be in the Little Miss Ugly pageant. Will you do it?" I said, "Yeah, I'll do it for you guys. Don't worry about it." I had to dress up like a girl and sing "Torn" by Natalie Umbriglia. I went shopping, bought a dress, heels, a green wig, etc. I memorized the song and practiced it, and then I thought I'd have some fun with it.

I got some Xanax from Garrett and went on stage, so I'm xannied out, and I just let loose. My voice is carrying across this whole giant auditorium, and I'm strutting around the stage in heels with my green wig. I'm trying to sing in falsetto but my voice keeps cracking, and I'm looking very sexy in my tight white dress! The audience is going wild...I'm like the star act of the pageant, and I just killed it. At one point in the song, the lyrics are "I don't miss her all that much..." and then I screamed out, "Beth!", and the audience erupted, just blew up, because all the girls and most of the audience knew about her and me, so it was hilarious, except Beth didn't think so and she ran out of the theater embarrassed and crying. All her friends and sisters were laughing and it was a huge moment. I kept on singing and toward the end I yanked off my green wig, threw it up in the air, and the audience screamed again. It was awesome! Cheese and Muggs recorded me doing my act, and the Little Miss Ugly video is on my YouTube channel. I sang this song pretty much for Beth, and on the video you can see Beth running out of the auditorium. You should check it out. After the show we went to the Luxe Bar to celebrate and hang out. Me, Muggs, Cheese, and Cohen were doing lines all night, and later on I got laid by one of Beth's friends.

Then I went through a rough patch because soon after that, my dad almost died. I got a call from my mom that my dad couldn't breathe and he was rushed to the hospital. Dad had to have surgery to place a ring valve in his heart. It was a very scary time for me. I don't know if this ever happened to you, but when one of your parents is in serious trouble and you might lose your dad or your mom, it really trips your mind. The thought of losing my dad was very hard to take. Luckily my dad wound up beating the surgery, but it was an awful few weeks until we knew he would survive. I'd just lost my grandmother not too long ago, and now the idea of losing my dad was almost too much.

My dad's illness and surgery brought Muggs and me closer together... Muggs had lost his dad before starting college so he knew what it was like, and he was able to be there for me and talk me through all the flooding emotions. Cheese, Lexington, Heather and Princess were also looking out for me. After my dad's successful surgery and recovery, they held a party and baked a cake for my dad. I was totally grateful for their support and friendship when I was struggling.

After I got through that and I was back at JWU, Muggs got a call from the police. Remember Muggs's Lexus was stolen in freshman year? We're hanging out smoking shit and things, and the cops call. "Like, hey, man, did you have a blue Lexus?" So Muggs goes, "Yeah, it got stolen about two and a half years ago. What the fuck is going on?" And they go like, "Well, we found it." He goes, "You found it? What do you mean, you found it?" So we go to the auto body shop, and it was like crazy. It didn't even look like a Lexus. Muggs had put about $22,000 worth of shit into this car and everything was stripped out of it. It was fucking crazy. That's how it ended, with the insurance company owning it now. They were just letting him see if there was anything in the car he wanted to get, even though nothing was left. They had already paid him for the Lexus; that junk heap wasn't even his car anymore.

Senior year was just a lot of sex, you know? I was catching up on girls that I hadn't had sex with yet, trying to hit my number, and I was trying to slay everything. There was a lot of going out and partying. We hung out at a club called Whiskey Republic. It's like an Irish waterfront sports bar sort of thing right on the river in Providence harbor. We would also go over to the Colosseum which was another banging place. I was hanging out with the little kids, like Mark and his twin brother, and Cohen, too. These were all the 'youngins', you know what I mean? They are all grown up now, but then they were freshmen and sophomores, the newbies. They were all cool kids, and it was fun showing the new kids the route to take, like the shit that we do, and how we fuck shit up, because I didn't get to meet them and show them how it's done when I was down in Miami.

We also went to a lot of raves. Alumni brothers were coming up, like Hanesworth and Steve Platinum ; they were all coming up to party and have a good time. I started rekindling the flame with a bunch of old friends and that was cool, reconnecting with all the dudes and their ladies. But then it was spring break, man, and me and Muggs decided we were going to go on vacation to Seattle.

Chapter 25

The Emerald City

I'd always wanted to live in Seattle. It's like this thing I had, you know? Something told me, from the time I was a little kid and I saw a map of the United States, I just always knew I'd live there.

Now that spring break was coming, I thought this would be a great time to run out there, check the scene, and start to visualize and materialize me living there after JWU. I kept saying I'm moving there, I'm moving there, I'm moving there, and Muggs was, pretty much, "Yo, fuck it, dude, I'm going to go with you," so Muggs wound up booking a ticket with me, and we went out there to have fun. But I'm also looking for a place to live, checking the scene, and seeing if I was going to like this city. I wound up liking it a lot, and everything went well. Muggs was going to move out with me, but in the end he wound up bailing on me.

Everywhere I said I was going to live or everything I said I wanted to do, I've done it, so I came out to Seattle just to do it. Muggs and me came out to the Pacific Northwest at break and we fucked this place up.

Slick and Muggs take Seattle! From the time we got off the plane until the time we left, it was one great party. Muggs's boy from home, Michael, who now lives in Corvallis, he came up to see us. We got together and were fucking shit up, and we pretty much brought Providence to the Emerald City. We were doing everything like at home, just without the Xans.

We hit every club possible. We hated the food at first, and the city smelled like hippies. It smelled sweaty and nasty and the food had the same smell. If you know the East Coast, it smelled like how the trains smell, musty and grimy, just like hippies that haven't washed.

We went to the UW campus to party and also explored the city; it's a pretty exciting place. Bell Town, Capitol Hill, the waterfront…all kinds of great clubs and a freaking ton of coffee shops. We climbed around on the Space Needle, went to the aquarium at the docks, visited the art museum, the Jimi Hendrix museum, smoked blunts, rode around the whole area and totally loved Pike Place Market where the fish guys throw the fish around for tourists. Once we got the lay of the land, the food got better, the drinks got stiffer, and the girls got friendlier. It was an awesome time!

But the whole time we're here, we get these breakdown messages from Cheese. If you remember, Buck, AKA Greg Buckley, who was Cheese's Marine friend from Hawaii, had died in August. Even though it's about six months ago, Cheese was still feeling this loss deeply. Buck was killed in Afghanistan by a deranged Afghan policeman who turned against several Marines in a restaurant there.

So, like, Cheese was telling us, "I'm going to kill myself." And it was just crazy, very weird, Cheese going off the deep end. I remember just sitting there, me and Muggs, looking at these messages, like, damn, what's happening? Cheese was ready to let himself go, you know what I mean?

Muggs was thinking that Cheese was just being gay. I'm sitting there kind of like, "Damn dude, I feel kind of bad for him." He just lost his best friend; Buck had just died that summer right before senior year. I had almost lost my dad, so I understood where he was coming from.

When we got back from Seattle, Muggs finally got his driver's license back. His license had been suspended since November when he was drunk the night before Halloween, crashed his car, popped off his tires, and broke it with Rainstorm.

Now St. Patty's Day came around, so I had a huge banger at my crib in the morning before the bar crawl with about 150 people in my apartment, solid, at all times. I had a couple of kegs, I made everybody steak and eggs, bagels and shit, and we had a great time!

That night Chuck and Cheese got into a fight. So Cheese's friend, Lexington, she wanted to go on the bar crawl with us. Well, Cheese didn't want her to go. I had already been through this whole thing with Beth before, so I'm telling him, "Cheese, like, dude, let Alexa come on the bar crawl with you. It's like nothing. She's not going to say anything if you're with any other girl." And he winds up saying, "No, she can't go." So then Alexa was up for staying with my cousin Chuck, and Cheese got mad, and he says, "Fuck that, she's coming with me!"

Later on that night words came up about it, and these two started to go at it. I mean, Cheese is throwing cups of water with Dutch gut in it at Chuck, and I'm looking at Chuck and thinking, like, when are you going to get up and knock this kid out? You know? It fucking finally hit him, so my cousin got up and they just started scrapping it out, and my cousin fucked him up. I'm not getting involved in this, you know, because that's my boy, and that's my cousin; let these two scrap it out, you know what I mean? They're both family, and they're both brothers, so whatever.

After this I didn't see Cheese for quite awhile. He was on this like, suicidal kind of thing. I felt he was ready to kill himself every day. Like he had a conversation with me on St. Patty's Day, and he would say such shit like, "Aw, man, you and Muggs are too close." It was kind of odd and weird to me, you know? I was like, "Dude, what do you mean?" He was like, "You're hanging with Muggs a lot." And I was, like, "Why are you mad about that?" You know? That sounded kind of gay to me, but whatever. But he was my boy, and I talked to him a lot and talked him down from the ledge, and he seemed fixed up.

I think I finally figured it out, though. Because me and Muggs went out to Seattle without him, and me and Muggs were so tight all the time since the Katina break-up back in November, Cheese thought I wasn't there for him anymore. He didn't have much money, so he was kind of stuck in this emotional soup. When you hang with people who have money, it's easy to keep falling on your face trying to keep up, you know what I mean? I sensed this was what was going on for Cheese, that Cheese felt left out and abandoned. Cheese had lost his best friend, Buck, didn't have any cash, and he couldn't keep up with us, and now he thought he was also losing me, so life was shit.

But then Cheese got serious with this girl, Alexa, and that helped relieve a lot of his anxiety. Alexa was tall and really well-built, you know? It's like how did Cheese, who we always thought might be gay, ever attract this totally awesome looking, stacked Mama? Cheese and Lexington were always together, and that's what I was telling him, like, "Yo, man, you might as well keep her, dude. Like it's not like you see a bunch of chicks every day, you know? You're not doing what I'm doing, and you're not doing what anyone else is doing. I would keep this girl, yo. She's been with you by your side. When you ain't going out with us, we've taken her out while you stayed in, so she's part of our crew now, you know, and she knows our lingo. She's a keeper for you, dude."

Our crew spoke in lipogram. We took the first letter off each word so only we understood each other, and most other people wouldn't understand us, you know what I mean? And his girl already understood our lingo, she was down, and...guess what? They're still together. That was awesome. I don't know how intimate they were or anything, but whatever. Cheese needed that. She was his company. She really was his girl.

Then there was this girl, Kait M, from freshman year. She threw a formal for our class, the Class of 2013, at Vanity. Usually the Greek organizations are the only groups that have formals, but Kait wanted to do one for everyone. Kait was part of our Washington Avenue crew. She hung out with Rainstorm, Marie and Linda, and she was an amazing party thrower. She always threw the craziest parties; that was a fact. She made sure she had permits from the state in case of noise complaints, always had more booze than needed and would have a round-two party the day after just to get rid of the excess alcohol. Kait knew how to have fun, and she was just awesome.

The formal required that we bring a date from our freshman year, so now I'm going with the biggest whore, Jo Jo the Ho Ho! I was one of the first ones to fuck her at school, but after that, I mean, all of us hit that. You know what I mean? So I'm going to this formal with this girl that I really haven't seen since freshman year. And that was kind of awkward. I'd been trying to stay away from her, and shit, now I was asking her out, so I felt kind of bad, but whatever. Yes, you're right...I had a good night with her!

I wanted to take Jenna, one of my ex-flings who I have all the love in the world for, but Jmass had a BF. I knew taking Jo Jo would rekindle the freshman year flame and I knew Jo Jo was down for whatever.

But now, back to Cheese and Biscuit. They're into their third fight. We were all going out one night, and something happened that pissed off Biscuit, so Biscuit kicked everybody out of his apartment. It was something about borrowing an auxiliary cord for a laptop. So Cheese and Biscuit were arguing, and Cheese kicked his door as Biscuit was trying to shut it...and the slamming door nearly cut off the top part of Biscuit's finger! Biscuit's finger was just flapping, so me and Cheese took him to the hospital to get it sewn back on or something.

When we got to the emergency room, it was jammed with broken-up people and there was a three or four hour wait! I couldn't stick around because I had a job interview and had to scram. I told Cheese to stay with Biscuit. I mean, shit, it was the least Cheese could do because he was the reason Biscuit's finger tip was flapping around, you know? So I left Cheese there with Biscuit. Later I heard that Biscuit got hungry and sent Cheese out to get some food at the nearby convenience store. Biscuit gave Cheese his credit card and told him to bring back some food. Cheese took off and bought all kinds of stuff for himself with Biscuit's card…burgers and drinks and candy and chips and magazines and pie and whatever else he saw. He brought back only one hot dog, a small bag of chips, and a bottle of water for Biscuit. All on Biscuit's credit card! "Well," Cheese said later when I asked him what the fuck he was thinking, "I'm Jewish."

And on top of that, after Cheese dropped off Biscuit's measly (cold, dried out) hot dog, Cheese took off and left Biscuit in the emergency room all by himself with his smashed finger. And then Biscuit had to walk home after he was released.

Biscuit and Cheese wound up getting into these fights, and these kids were so soft that their boys would get into fights for them! Their boys had a huge brawl in my apartment one day, out of fucking nowhere, and they were ramming into things and breaking stuff, and I'm like, "Get the fuck out! And you two guys need to fight this out, not your fucking boys!" You know? And this wound up being an ongoing thing, I mean, Biscuit was calling the cops, and all this kind of shit. They couldn't leave each other alone, you know? Oil and water. It was crazy.

The next thing that happens is now P-Money and Muggs got into a fight. It's right before alumni weekend, and we went out one night and we're at this bar. Biscuit and Fowler were there with us. Fowler was another member of our crew but wasn't really around much. He wound up being roommates with P-Money and Serge during our senior year. Fowler's an Italian guido from Connecticut.

Muggs came into the bar talking shit, and this was an old roommate beef, you know? They've been roommates and they hated each other. It was just old Capricorn shit, man, and they wound up getting into it. P-Money punched Muggs in the face. I had just stepped out of the bar and told Biscuit and Fowler to keep things calm. Fowler was with P-Money, and then there was me, Biscuit and Muggs. And I told Biscuit to watch those two, and I'd be right back. I told P-Money not to touch him, but P-Money just slammed him. Right in the face.

Muggs was bleeding from his eye, and P-Money was kicked out of the bar while I was walking back from the ATM. Later the two dudes smoked a blunt and talked it out, but they still can't stand each other.

Chapter 26

The Boston Marathon Bombings

April 15, 2013. I was interning in Boston for my talent agency, but I don't really call it an internship because I didn't have to do shit. I was making a daily 45-minute trip from Providence to Boston, commuting daily. You know, get on the train with everybody else, get a newspaper and a coffee, watch the world go by as I sped along the tracks. It was a relaxing trip, the train swaying slightly, kind of like being in a cradle. There was an interesting variety of every-day people around me, all going to Boston like I was. A lot of these people did this every day, and would do it every day for 20 or 30 years. The idea was unsettling. It made me realize how different I was because there was no fucking way I was going to fall, or fail, into this pattern that millions of people lived every day, every year...for decades. Might as well be dead, you know? I mean, really, what did they have? Food on the table and weekends doing shit around the house. I knew there was something better. And so do you.

Anyway, I was done with school after the winter and knew I was graduating. I didn't really have to do anything else, so in the spring I interned.

I was modeling and doing acting at the time, like I still do, and my talent agency needed someone to file papers and do office shit for like two or three hours a day. I thought, what the hell, I'd help them out, and I'd have them sign-off on my college internship requirement so I wouldn't have to do shit-else. Also, in this way I'd be right on the spot when a job came through, and I'd get first dibs. I would just go in whenever I wanted, and leave whenever I wanted. I got to be behind the camera now instead of in front of it, filming people to see what that was like, and audition people, do some filing and organizing, and stuff like that. This way I also met a lot of people, which was fun, and you never knew who might walk in the front door.

When I got off the train that morning in Boston, I knew something was going to happen. It was freaky. I saw a lot of bomb squad trucks in front of the station. It was fucking crazy. So I'm like, damn, what the hell is going on? It didn't seem right, you know? It's like they knew something was going to happen. I lit up a cigarette and went to work, and then didn't think anything else about it.

When the bombs went off, I was indoors. I was watching a movie in the office while I was filing away some papers. Suddenly I heard BOOM – BOOM! And my buddy, Garrett, the computer nerd in my apartment building back in Providence, texted me; and he wrote, "Dude, you better get out of there, two bombs just went off in Boston!"

My manager at the office didn't want to let me leave. He thought there would be more chaos and danger and wanted me to stay in the office building. And I was like fuck this! I hit up my buddy Joey and my buddy Jake, and I was, "Yo, I can't get out of here! Do you mind if I stay with you guys tonight?" Joey, Jake and Pat's dads run Boston. They're retired dudes and own the top five nightclubs and restaurants in Boston. My boys said yeah, but I wound up being able to get out after all.

When I got out of the office and onto the street, everything was scattered. There were people running around, and the streets were emptying. It was like weird; I'd never seen a city so empty before. I ran to the train station and caught the last train into Providence. I literally hopped on the train as the doors were closing.

Later I found out the bombing was just two blocks from my intern job. And the bombs went off right near where I usually eat lunch over by Pi Alley. First 9/11, and seeing this shit now... What the fuck?

Chapter 27

The Vacation's About Over

The hardest class I ever had in college was art. Me and Muggs took this class together. The teacher was literally failing everybody in class. It was like the history of art and stuff. So I went and talked to this lady and she said, "You guys aren't writing good enough papers." I said, "Lady, this isn't a fucking English class! It's fucking art, you know?"

Classes in my senior year were awesome. You knew the clock was winding down, and everything was going so much faster. It was kind of scary because I realized I'd never see these kids again, like every single day. I mean I'd see them, but it wouldn't be the same. And some of these kids I'd really never see again. So it was kind of bittersweet, knowing this was the end for so much. And though there was more to come, the thing was it would never be the same. It's like this chapter was closing. Yeah, yeah, a new one would start, but it didn't take away from the feeling that this great story was quickly coming to an end. Sometimes changes are good and there's no looking back...but sometimes changes are a mixed bag, silver lining and all that shit. The point is, it was going to be hard to say goodbye no matter how bright the next story was going to be, you know?

So there were a lot of chill-out parties, lots of smoking weed, and a lot of time just catching up with each other before the end came.

Right before senior year ended we had a couple of big raves. On Cinco de Mayo, a week before our graduation, DJ Thomas Gold came up. It was Linda's birthday, Trupps's ex-girlfriend with the big tits. She was walking around with these little sticky pink things on her nipples, and, like literally, her vagina showing. She's just wow! Linda and Marie are my two most favorite girls in college, part of my crew on Washington Street, for all the shit we went through. Those are my girls. And Rainstorm, too, Muggs's ex-girl. Even though we kind of fell off with her after she and Muggs broke up on Halloween.

Oh, yeah. There was this other thing going on in the last few weeks before graduation. I have to tell you this, about a chick named Irene. I had hooked up my buddy Garrett with his girl named Chloe. And Chloe was cool with this tall sexy blonde named Nika. Nika was just awesome, she was amazing, she came right off the boat from the Ukraine, and she was dating this kid I didn't really like. He was a lowly freshman, too, and I didn't like him, and I knew I was going to fuck her, like sometimes you can just tell it's going to happen, you know? Irene told me we should've fucked the weekend before because that's when we could both feel the strong physical attraction between us. She said, "Fuck it, we'll fuck tonight for sure!" We were going out to a bar with our crew, and Irene whispered, "I'm going to give you a signal, and when I do, find a way to leave and meet me outside." Okay...! So she gave me the signal and we left, and we got back to my apartment in no time at all. Nika stripped naked and she had this gorgeous ass and big full breasts, long blonde hair, and she was eager to play! So I got busy and fucked her, and this chick pissed in my fucking bed!

Even so, that was like the best pussy ever. She was awesome, and we exercised together a lot after that, if you know what I mean. Funny story, her boyfriend came up to me one time and goes, "You know, man, I'm really happy you and Nika are such good friends. I heard her say she likes your house a lot." And I'm just looking at this kid like he's fucking retarded because I'm like, dude, your girl is not staying at my house to play checkers! You know what I mean? I'm clearly fucking her, you know? That's how I'm looking at him, but whatever. I just let him think me and his girl were just friends.

On alumni weekend I was too xannied out to do anything. It occurred to me that this time next year...I'd be one of the alumni! Holy shit! With all these thoughts and feelings flooding through me, I was like xannied out of my mind. I was like passed out, knocked out, sleeping and shit, you know? I don't remember alumni weekend, except that Biscuit had brought his boys up from Chicago, and Biscuit wanted to settle accounts for all the hassle with the apartment wars and losing the top of his middle finger...his fucking middle finger, man! It's hard giving someone the finger when part of it is missing, you know? You have to use the other hand... Biscuit was being real tough, looking for Cheese. He wanted him and his boys to fuck up Cheese, you know? "Yeah, we'll fuck up Cheese and we'll fuck up Cheese's boys!" And all that dumb shit. That was all fucked up. Cheese was off somewhere with Alexa so this never played out the way Biscuit wanted.

But now it's almost graduation time! The last couple of weeks were real hectic. It was like oh, shit! We're getting our caps and gowns, we're going out to get new outfits, we're taking pictures and all that kind of stuff. The night before graduation, my parents came up and it seemed everybody's families were here; it was like crazy with all the 'rents around! It was so weird because they didn't belong here, all at the same time, on our turf, you know? It only made everything even stranger…because now the real world was starting to reappear and take over again.

On the day of graduation I was still hammered from the night before, and I was passed out. Everyone was supposed to be gathered at the freakin' Dunkin' Donuts Center for the commencement ceremony at 8 a.m., which was just fucking stupid! Who thinks this stuff up? And my buddy Gabe, who was one of Biscuit's boys, he came upstairs to my apartment and broke in and got me up. He threw me in the shower, locked the door on me, and told me to wake up. I started crying, man, because it was all over! I like chugged a whole bottle of Grand Marnier, well, not the whole bottle, but I was chugging from the bottle, listening to the song "One More Time" by Daft Punk:

> "One more time
> We're gonna celebrate
> Oh yeah, all right
> Don't stop the dancing…"

...over and over and over, and it was just awesome, you know, knowing that this time was now done, and it was over. Over... Fucking over. Over forever.

So now I'm wasted, I have to get all dolled up, and I have to get my ass over to the Dunkin' Donuts Center. For those of you who don't know the Dunkin' Donuts Center in Providence, it's like this huge arena. It's a giant venue for sports games, New England dog shows, monster truck exhibitions and all kinds of shit, including our graduation. They have this giant jumbotron, skyscraper-sized speakers, and the ceiling is like massive...like the Superdome or some such shit, you know? Well, maybe not that big, but pretty fucking big!

Somehow I got dressed and got my graduation robe and cap, and made it to the Center. I saw all my bros and crew who are graduating with me, you know, and we're all hungover and disbelieving we're actually here, that the time has come; and then we take our seats, and one by one the rows of kids are called up to walk across the stage, get their diploma and shake the Dean's hand...all very standard.

But this was huge. When I was called to cross the stage, the whole auditorium burst out in applause! Everybody pretty much went-off with my name, and I'm like screaming along with them! The whole place just exploded! I looked out at all the kids, people I'd known for four years, kids who had bought drugs from me, got drunk with me, fought with me, had sex with me, done crazy shit with me, brothers, sisters, thousands of them, and they were all yelling my name, fist-pumping, laughing and celebrating for me! It was crazy! And I didn't even get a chance to shake the Dean's hand.

I'll never forget that day, you know what I mean? Afterwards there were a bunch of girls and they came running up to me and said, "Like, yo, Vic! We know you couldn't hear us but we were screaming for you! We love you!" It was awesome and I felt like a fucking celebrity. It was definitely a great feeling.

That was pretty much where things stood. The last hurrah was at the View Lounge in Waterplace Park with views of the city skyline and waterfront. There were about 3,000 of us there, 3,000 people raving it up all night long. We had about two ounces of coke, and me, Muggs, Muggs's sister, and Muggs's two boys did lines all night. Me and Muggs, back to drugs. Muggs's boys call me White Muggs, and they call him Black Vic. You know what I mean? It's kind of funny! That night we had massive amounts of drugs, just to cope with all the feelings. We partied until the next fucking morning. And then, by morning, everybody was gone, pretty much.

Kind of upsetting, watching my boy Garrett move out that day. This was the kid who would leave his apartment door open for me, like, if he was going home for the weekend or he was going somewhere, he would leave his door open so I could go in and hang out in his apartment if I got bored in mine, you know? And vice versa. That's how we all were, me, him and Biscuit. It was just fucked up because it was all over.

It turns out that these four years were really very short, and I could do them all over again with those same kids. It's amazing how much we accomplished and how much we actually grew up. Totally...fucking...amazing.

Chapter 28

Shout Out

To my mom and my dad, thank you from the bottom of my heart. None of this would have happened if it wasn't for you, you know? Thank you, working as hard as you did to send me to college and let me have these experiences. I want you to know my appreciation for busting your ass and dealing with me all your lives, with all the trouble I've been into.

I want to thank the friends I first met at orientation, Hannah, Brandon, Doudji, Andrew, Sarah, Katie, and Lindsay. We stayed tight through everything, and no matter how hard times got, and even though we didn't always hang out together and may have skipped a year or so, whatever, but like I said, at the end of the day we all still came together.

I want to thank my fraternity brothers and sorority sisters, you know, because it was definitely an awesome ride. Being your brother taught me more than I could have learned on my own in twice the time. You are an awesome group of great people. Much love!

And then, to my best friends in college: I want to say thanks to the Washington Street crew, because without you, this book wouldn't be possible; together we built this story.

I want you to know this isn't just my book; this is the Class of 2013's book. And this book also belongs to everyone else who knew me and enjoyed the time we had together at Johnson and Wales during my four years. Without you, this story wouldn't have come to light.

For the people who didn't get in the book, you all get honorable mention. If I appear to have left you out, it isn't so. Don't worry because I'll be writing a couple of sequels to this book; this book is nowhere near finished. This right here is just to get the juicy shit out! I'm going to go back and touch on the details in the next couple of books…so watch for your story to be told here, too.

For the kids out there who have the opportunity to go to college, just go! You know, go get it done. It's a once in a lifetime deal. I'm not telling anyone to do what I did in this book, but I just want to show people these are the hardships that happen in college, these are the things that you have to overcome, and this is the shit that makes you a man or a woman today.

If you can't finish in four years, it's not an issue, bro, because there are things that happen in life that may require you to step back, you know? As long as you go in and you get it done and you meet new people and you have a story to tell, you've done the right thing. Whether all you get is your freshman year, or you make it through the sophomore, junior or senior years, if you've built relationships, you've networked, you've had troubles, you've hung on through the ups and downs, then you've graduated, to me...whether you're in college for one year or five years, whatever it may be.

For you parents, I want you to know this is not all that your kids are doing, you know? We may appear to be degenerates in college, but don't look at us like this is how we're going to be when we graduate, or when we start our careers. I'm letting you know these are the things that go on in your kids' lives, so when you're yelling at your kid, also have some leniency because this is the shit they're dealing with on the other side, the things they have to go through and live with. These are shark infested waters, you know?

This is also a shout out for the inner city kids who didn't have much, but who still made it to college. I give you the biggest props because when you come from the hardships of life, that right there makes you a strong person. Nothing but respect for you!

No matter what, every single person I went to Johnson and Wales with, or that I interacted with in Providence, no matter what, you are my brother or my sister; you're my family. You don't have to be in a fraternity or sorority, you don't have to be or do anything. If we've come across each other during those four quick years in Rhode Island, you mean something special to me, and you're my family, more my family than anything else.

The name of this book is the "Best Four Year Vacation Ever!" and this was a short vacation, and I feel another four years still wouldn't have been enough. We need a lifetime together! All of us created these rich experiences.

That's the other thing. It wasn't about the learning in the classroom. We learned from those around us. I learned from my peers; I didn't learn shit from the books. All the books had were fucking blank pages. You know? We learned from those around us, and that's what made us successful. We had to make friends, we had to break friends, we had to leave friends, we got in trouble together, you know, we did it all, so many trials and tribulations, and we all stuck through it.

I came to college and I met everybody. And I didn't just meet everyone at Johnson and Wales, I met everyone in Rhode Island and became a famous person there. I even had my own fucking sandwich named after me! And I wasn't a fake person. I always stayed true to my own, true to myself.

Farewell for now, Johnson and Walers, Class of 2013 ... and I will see you all at the top!

Chapter 29

The Meaning of Life

So here's what I believe.

Be true to yourself. Find those who are close with you and won't give up on you.

Go out and do everything and be everything you want to be. America is a great place, and we've got freedom, man, so go out and do everything you can because tomorrow you might not wake up.

Step away from all the patterns and all the shit that slows you down, step away from all that shit and guide your own path. Just be you. Don't be someone else just because this or that person is cool and has tattoos. Don't go out and get that shit if that's not you, you know what I mean? When you wake up in the morning and say, "I want to sail across the fucking river", go fucking build a boat and go fucking sail across it! You know what I mean? If I say I'm going somewhere and I'm going to do something, I'm going there and doing it no matter fucking what, you know?

I came out to Seattle with only 1,500 fucking dollars in my account, which was graduation money. That's all I had left and I moved out here and fucking built a whole life. I built myself up from the bottom, and I've never really ever been at the bottom before. So it was awesome to do that, all on my own, without my parents. My parents are always there for me, you know what I mean? My parents will help me out with anything in life. But I told them, "This right here is the time for you to step down and let me handle this shit." And I did all this shit on my own. I put all this shit together on my own, and I feel fucking awesome about this!

So that's my thing in life: don't let people do it for you; just go out and get this shit done yourself. Wake up, be spontaneous, get it the fuck done, don't hurt others, and have a good time. And if you're feeling really down and shit, you know what? Shake it off, don't throw any salt on it, maybe catch your breath if you need to, and then go out there and kill it.

Do what the hell makes you happy.

Your bro, Victor Slicktor.

99 Bodies but 100 Wasn't One

1. Alaina
2. Alli
3. Ally
4. Alyssa W
5. Amanda B
6. Amber
7. Ana S
8. Anabell
9. Ariel P
10. Ashley K.
11. Ashley M
12. Beautiful
13. Bianca
14. Bianca M
15. Britt
16. Brittany
17. Brittany T
18. Cammy
19. Carolina
20. Cassandra D
21. Cayley
22. Chelsea
23. Chelsea
24. Chelsea
25. Courtney
26. Courtney
27. Courtney S
28. Crystal B
29. Domonique C
30. Ellen M
31. Emily
32. Emily F.
33. Falon
34. Gianna
35. Hayley D
36. HeatherV
37. Holly
38. Irene
39. J Mass
40. Jackie M
41. Jade
42. Janine
43. Jenna F.
44. Jill
45. Johanna
46. Kaitlyn
47. Kate J
48. Kate R
49. Katie S
50. Kelly
51. Ki
52. Kristin
53. Krystal
54. Lala
55. Lauren
56. Lilivette
57. Linnea
58. Lisa
59. Luisa
60. Mandie
61. MarissaM
62. Mary
63. Mckenzie
64. Melissa
65. Monique
66. Montoya
67. Natalie
68. Olivia L
69. Paige
70. Rachel
71. Sade
72. Sam Jo Ann
73. Samantha R
74. Sarah S
75. Sasha Q
76. Shailey
77. Shannon
78. Shelby
79. Stacey
80. Stacey
81. Steph
82. Stephanie
83. SugarTits
84. Sydny
85. Taylor
86. Teria
87. Theresa
88. Tina
89. Toni
90. Tory
91. Traci
92. Valerie
93. Vanessa
94. Victoria
95. Victoria
96. Wendy
97. Yaritza
98. Yaz
99. Yesenia

Where We Are Today

Slicktor Victor - After college, I moved to Seattle to grab my dream career in the sales and marketing field. After about two weeks of working corporate, I decided to start my own business with the funds I had left over. Now that I'm almost a year with my company, I'm ready for my next move to Los Angeles in June.

Muggs - After college, Muggs had a DUI accident; yeah, I know, AGAIN, but he pulled through and is currently studying for his Series 7 test to become a financial accountant.

**P$** - Even though P$ didn't graduate with our class of 2013 like he was supposed to, he is now a real estate sales agent in NYC dealing in commercial buildings.

Cheese - Cheese is currently still trying to start his own cooking show, "KWK". He is currently working as a front desk attendant for the Marriott Hotel of Central Park, as well as casting for various cooking shows.

Turbs - Turbs has recently started his own construction business in Manhattan.

Trups - Trups is a marketing assistant manager for a corporation in Denver, Colorado that handles all of the huge events in the state.

Milla - Milla is currently a Sous Chef in Denver, Colorado looking to make his next move further west to San Diego.

Wii Fii - Wii dropped out of college during our senior year since he wasn't really making progress in school. He recently has come out of the closet and labels himself as a gay rapper.

Rainstorm - Works as a daily assistant for a horse racing track on Long Island, New York.

Linda - After getting her boob job done, Linda landed a job as a Hooters waitress in Westchester, New York.

Marie - Marie landed a job a few months after graduation doing administrative support in Boston, Massachusetts.

From degenerates to corporates!

www.ingramcontent.com/pod-product-compliance
Lightning Source LLC
Chambersburg PA
CBHW031415290426
44110CB00011B/388